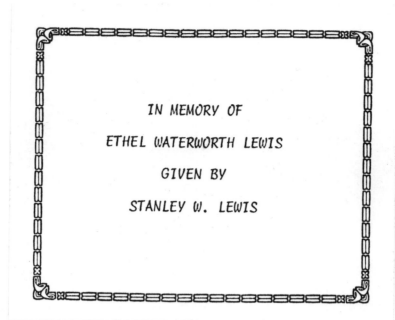

IN MEMORY OF

ETHEL WATERWORTH LEWIS

GIVEN BY

STANLEY W. LEWIS

# EARLY
# NEW ENGLAND
# GRAVESTONE
# RUBBINGS

*by Edmund Vincent Gillon, Jr.*

*Dover Publications, Inc., New York*

Published in Canada by General Publishing
Company, Ltd., 30 Lesmill Road, Don Mills,
Toronto, Ontario.

Published in the United Kingdom by Constable and
Company, Ltd., 10 Orange Street, London W. C. 2.

*Early New England Gravestone Rubbings* is a new
work, first published by Dover Publications, Inc.,
in 1966.

This volume belongs to the Dover "Pictorial Archive
Series"; it is sold with the understanding that illustrations may be reproduced for advertising or edi-
torial purposes without payment or special permission. Such permission is, however, limited to the use
of not more than ten illustrations in any single
publication. Please address the publisher for permission to make more extensive use of illustrations
in this volume. The publisher will appreciate the
usual credit line, indicating title, author and publisher, although such credit is not a requirement
for use.

*Library of Congress Catalog Card No.: 66-14555*

Manufactured in the United States of America
Dover Publications, Inc.
180 Varick Street
New York, N. Y. 10014

# PREFACE

The purpose of this book is one of pictorial documentation rather than the presentation of a scholarly text. I wish merely to call attention to the remarkable variety of early New England gravestones, the originality of the men who carved them, and the quality of their work. However, in the interest of scholarship I have prepared an appendix of notes on the plates in which I try to explain some of the symbols that appear on the slabs, make stylistic identifications and, in a few instances, attribute workmanship to particular stonecutters. The rubbings reproduced here were made over a period of years, and my notes covering this work are unfortunately incomplete, but where such information is available I have also given the location of the stone and the date, if no date appears on the rubbing itself.

Since virtually all the rubbings had to be greatly reduced for the format of this book, I have also prepared a table of the widths of the actual rubbings at their widest point, so that the reader will perhaps be able to visualize the true size of the stones depicted.

The reader whose interest in early New England gravestones goes beyond the scope of this book is referred to Harriette M. Forbes' authoritative study, *Gravestones of Early New England* (Boston, 1927), a work which contains a wealth of information about the actual men who carved the stones.

# CONTENTS

Reader
Keep death & Judgment
allway's in your eye
Non's fitt to live
But who is fitt to die

# INTRODUCTION

In the early burying grounds of New England a unique expression of primitive art exists, which has received scant recognition by the art historian and has gone relatively unnoticed by a public familiar with most other aspects of our national heritage. This unheralded wealth of material is to be found in the carved designs on the tombstones, which stand not only as monuments to the individuality of the deceased, but also as testimonials to the innate sense of design and excellent craftsmanship of the stone-cutters who produced them. These stone slabs with their brooding death's-heads, winged cherubs, stylized portraits, and willows and urns, are reflections of the religious beliefs, philosophy, and fashion of their time. Our appreciation of them may be heightened by a basic knowledge of the spirit in which they were created.

The earliest markers erected by the Puritans reflected an attitude toward death which differed considerably from that of later generations. To a people who suffered the rigors of a severe climate, famine, and epidemics, death was a fearsome prospect. So it is not surprising to see carved on their stones images of the grim reaper snuffing out the candle of life, or hollow-eyed grinning skulls beckoning to the passerby with the popular epitaph:

> AS YOU ARE NOW,
> SO ONCE WAS I;
> AS I AM NOW,
> SO YOU MUST BE.
> SO PREPARE FOR DEATH
> AND FOLLOW ME.

Only the world beyond the grave held the promise of a more comfortable life. Thus, the perpendicular stone borders of this early period were carved with motifs symbolizing heavenly rewards: figs and pomegranates denoted prosperity and happiness, the rope expressed eternity, and the rising sun was a symbol of the soul's resurrection. The grave-yard, especially when it was in proximity to the meeting house, served as a place of contemplation and instruction during the recess between the morning and afternoon sermons of the Sabbath. In an age when illiteracy was not uncommon, the monuments of this period relied heavily on such symbolism to convey their messages of the mortality of man and the blessings of Heaven.

In the eighteenth century, when the sternness of the Puritan faith lessened somewhat, the tombstones were embellished with less formidable motifs. The skulls and crossbones, full skeletons and empty hourglasses became less ubiquitous and were slowly supplanted by winged cherubs, a subject which evolved into angels and finally into a stylized type of portraiture. In the depiction of the angel it is often difficult to determine whether the portrayal is actually meant to be an angel or a representation of the deceased. The early portrait stones frequently record details of costume and indicate the station in life or occupation of the deceased.

The last important development in the three centuries of early gravestone design was the influence of the architectural motifs of the Federal and Greek Revival periods. This influence was reflected in delicate classical urns, medallions, and graceful swags, subjects which adorned fences and mantels of the region's more elaborate buildings. The most popular mortuary decoration was the willow tree, introduced into America in the first half of the eighteenth century. The stonecutter often depicted the willow and urn on full entablatures supported by Doric, Corinthian, Ionic, or Tuscan pilasters. There was a rather free interpretation of these orders, and the capitals were often handled with distinct originality.

The last period of early tombstone design ended with a decline in craftsmanship and a taste for the eclectic. Consequently, it is at this juncture that it seems esthetically appropriate to terminate this brief history of the art of of New England's gravestones.

# The Stonecutters

Having established that religious philosophy and fashion influenced the design of New England's early gravestones, the question then arises who the men were who carved them. Because the region's early population was relatively sparse, the business of stonecutting could hardly have provided anyone with a sufficient source of income. Therefore an artisan engaged in such an enterprise would of necessity be compelled to ply other trades, such as masonry or the slating of roofs. Another craftsman so engaged might have been the cordwainer, who not only made and repaired shoes, but also produced more ornamental leather items such as wallets, powder pouches, saddles, and chair seats. These required fine tooled work, and it is not unlikely that the details of design used on them were borrowed for the decoration of tombstones. The brazier and woodcarver most probably found himself recruited as a stonecutter, and the influences of these crafts are evident in the stones created.

With the growth of population the business of providing gravestones became a trade in which men could become exclusively engaged for a livelihood. As a result of the apprenticeship system practiced at that time, there emerged throughout the New England area families of stonecutters whose craft was plied through several generations. Deeds, probate records, inventory accounts, sometimes signatures on the stones themselves, reveal some of the names of men who actively engaged in this craft. Even the work of stonecutters whose names are still anonymous has been tabulated on the basis of stylistic configurations. But whether these men be known to us or not, their stones display a rich variety of design and a remarkable degree of originality.

# The Rubbings

The method chosen to best illustrate the strong graphic quality of New England gravestones is a technique referred to as rubbing. There are various ways of making rubbings, but I will describe only the method I have found to be most satisfactory in terms of faithful reproduction, simplicity and speed. This method also allows one to strengthen weak rubbings and, frequently, to complete rubbings taken from stones that are chipped or partially defaced.

It is hoped that anyone who admires the striking designs of early tombstones and cares enough to acquire his own collection of rubbings will be helped in doing so by the following suggestions.

The required materials are few and may be purchased at any art supply store: a roll of masking tape, a large pad or roll of strong bond paper, and a box of black lumber-marking wax crayons.

The first step in making a rubbing is to clean the stone of lichen, dirt and other foreign matter. Next, carefully tape the paper to the stone, making sure that the paper clings tightly, since the slightest shift will cause a blurring of the design. Finally, remove the wrapper from the crayon and lightly rub the broad edge of the crayon over the entire surface of the paper, thus establishing the over-all pattern. That part of the stone which touches the underside of the paper will be recorded in black, and that part which is recessed—the incised design—will be represented by the white areas.

Once the over-all design areas have been established, it is necessary to rub again with a firmer pressure, this time working in from the edges which separate the surface of the stone from the depressed background.

The character of the rubbing depends partly on the texture of the stone. Slate yields the greatest contrast in the image, whereas sandstone produces the coarsest texture. Schist and marble prove the least satisfactory.

A weak contrast in a rubbing due to the rough texture of the stone may be corrected after the removal of the paper by touching up the black areas with a crayon. This procedure is effected with a smoother stone surface, such as a piece of slate, under the paper. In this way an almost imperceptible design can be made to stand out clearly.

# The Photographs

Gravestone decoration represents one of the most difficult and subtle forms of sculpture, that of low relief carving. The sculptor, confined to a working depth of a fraction of an inch, is challenged with the carving of forms that not only capture the spiritual quality of the subject, but also create the illusion of lifelike full-bodied round-ness. Many designs owe part of their success to the optical phenomenon created by light striking the oblique incision at a different angle than the parent surface, thus causing the incision to appear nearly white against the darker surface. When low relief sculp-ture is reproduced in the form of a rubbing, the result is strikingly unlike the subject that it is taken from. The most dramatic difference is that embossed areas become divorced from the background, creating a design that is no longer linear but rather one consisting of broad patterns.

The selection of photographs at the end of this volume will give the reader a more exact idea of what the gravestones actually look like, and will also perhaps illustrate better than do the rubbings the tactile qualities and surface textures of early New England grave-stones. A comparison between a rubbing and a photograph (Plates 44 and 179, bottom) re-veals the marked difference in the nature of the two mediums. A number of interesting stones which are too fully sculptured to be rubbed are also illustrated in this section.

# Death's-Heads, Angels & Portraits

*Plate 1*

*Plate 2*

DEPOSITED
Beneath this Stone the Mortal Part
of Mr.s SUSANNA JAYNE, the amiable Wife of
Mr. PETER JAYNE, who lived Beloved
and Died Universally Lamented, on
August 8.th 1776 in the 45.th
Year of her Age.

Plate 3

*Plate 4*

*Plate 5*

*Plate 6*

In Memory of
Miſs MARY NORTON
Daughter of
BERIAH NORTON Esqʳ
& ANNFRANCES his Wife
Departed this Life
Sepᵗ. 23ᵈ. 17 81.
Aged 86 Years.

*Plate 7*

*Plate 8*

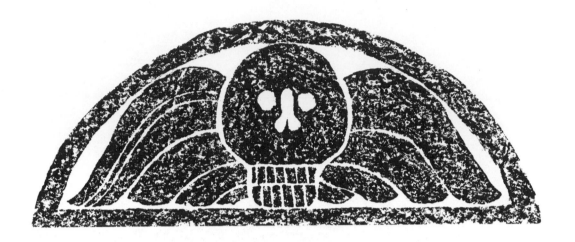

*Plate 9*

*Plate 10*

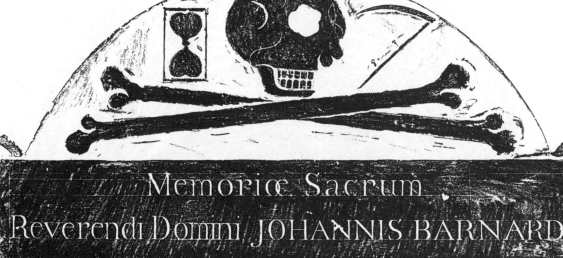

Memoriæ Sacrum
Reverendi Domini JOHANNIS BARNARD
primæ Christi Ecclesiæ apud MARBLEHEAD
Pastoris fidelis.___Theologus erat vire
eruditus Concionator admodum sapiens
utilisque suis non solum quin & posteris
monita reliquit Exemplumpietatis ac

*Plate 11*

Here lies Inter'd the Remains of the
Respectable ELISHA LYON Eldest Son of
Cap.t NEHEMIAH LYON, & MEHETABLE his
wife. HE. died OCT. 15.th 1767. in the 24.th
Year of His Age. His Death is mournfully
memorable, on account of the manner and
Occasion. For as He was Decently going
thro the military manual Exercise, in the
Company under Comand of Cap.t ELISHA
CHILD. S.d Cap.t Giving the words of
Command. He was Wounded by the
discharge of Fire arms, used, by one of
the Company. S.d arms having been
Loaded Intirely unknown to him;
the wound was Instantaneous DEATH

Plate 12

*Plate 13*

Here lies the Remains of
M:ˢ SARAH BEACH, Wife to the
Rev.ᵈ M:ʳ JOHN BEACH, who after
having been a dutiful Child, a
loving Sifter, an amiable, & faithful
Wife, a tender & careful mother, a moft
devout Chriftian, exchanged this
Life for Immortality AUG:ᵗ 1ˢᵗ 1756.

*Plate 14*

*Plate 15*

*Plate 16*

Plate 17

*Plate 18*

*Plate 19*

In Memory of y͏ᵉ Rev͏ᵈ
Mr Solomon Pain͏ᵉ
Paſtor of a Congre-
gational Church of
Chriſt in Canterbur͏y
Who Departed Th͏ᵉ
Life Oct͏ʳ y͏ᵉ 25͏th
1754 in y͏ᵉ 57͏th Year

*Plate 20*

*Plate 21*

HERE LIES THE BODY OF
M.rs ELIZABETH BARNARD.

THE WIFE OF

M.r EBENEZER BARNARD;

SHE DIED AUGUST 4.th

1753: IN y.e 59.th YEAR

OF HER AGE.

*Plate* 22

*Plate 23*

HERE LIES Y BODY OF
CAP^tn. JONATHAN PAYSON,
HE DIED DECEMBER 23^D.
1760: AGED 82 YEARS

*Plate 24*

Sacred to the memory
of Mrs TEMPERANCE WILLIAMS
Confort of Mr ISRAEL WILLIAMS
And Daughter of
Dr DAVID HOLMES & TEMPERANCE his Wife

Adding lustre to an amiable character
By sustaining her last illness
With Christian resignation
She departed this life
March 20th 1795
Ætat. XXI.

The scythe of Time "cuts down
The fairest bloom of sublunary blifs."

Young

*Plate 25*

*Plate 26*

In memory of
Miss. Eunice Dean dau
of Mr. Simeon Dean,
& Tamesin his wife
who died March 1800
In her 24th Year

Affliction sore, long time I bore,
Physicians skill was vain,
Till God was pleas'd to give me ease,
And free me from thy pain.

Plate 27

*Plate 28*

*Plate 29*

PHILETUS Alfo TITUs
Son of EZ their Son
EKIEL and died Sept
MARY CO 13 1778 in
NKLING ye 2d year of
died Sept his Age
6 1778 in
ye 10th year
of his Age

*Plate* 30

*Plate 31*

Here lyes y Body of
Mary-Ann Foldick Daug
of Mr Thomas & Mrs Anna
Foldick Who Died Jan 11 1766
Aged 10 Months & 12 Days.

Save fruitless tears & weep no more
This Babe's not lost but gone before

Plate 32

*Plate 33*

In Memory of
M<sup>rs</sup> HULDAH PEIRCE
Wife of Cap SETH
PEIRCE ~
who died March
y 15<sup>th</sup> AD. 1793 In the
44<sup>th</sup> year of her
age ~

*Plate 34*

*Plate 35*

*Plate  36*

Plate 37

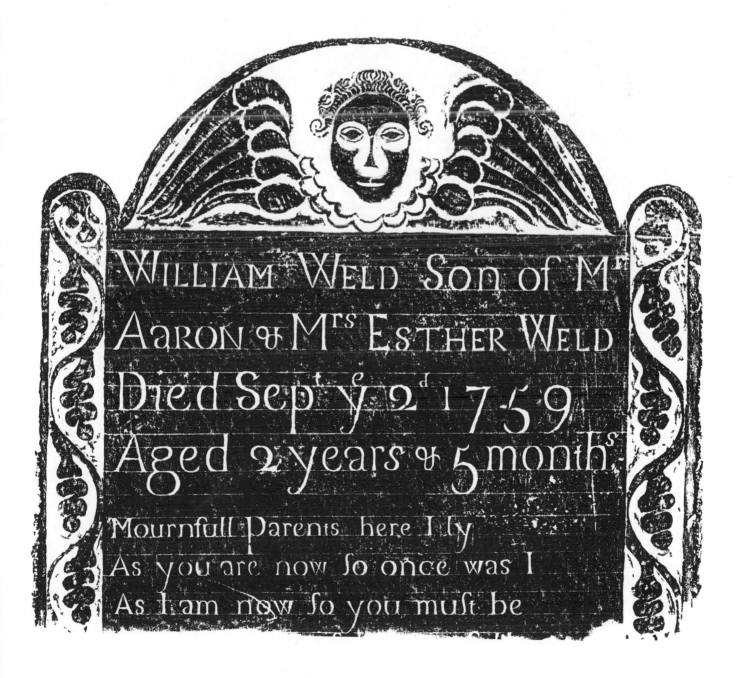

WILLIAM WELD Son of M<sup>r</sup>
AARON & M<sup>rs</sup> ESTHER WELD
Died Sep<sup>t</sup> y 2<sup>d</sup> 1759
Aged 2 years & 5 month<sup>s</sup>

Mournfull Parents here I ly
As you are now so once was I
As I am now so you must be

*Plate 38*

Plate 39

*Plate 40*

Plate 41

SACRED

to the memory of,

Mr TIMOTHY HARTSHORN

who died

July 13th 1800,

Aged 70 Years.

If virtue, honesty, and truth, coud save
He lives in realms of bliss far, far, beyond
the Grave.

*Plate 42*

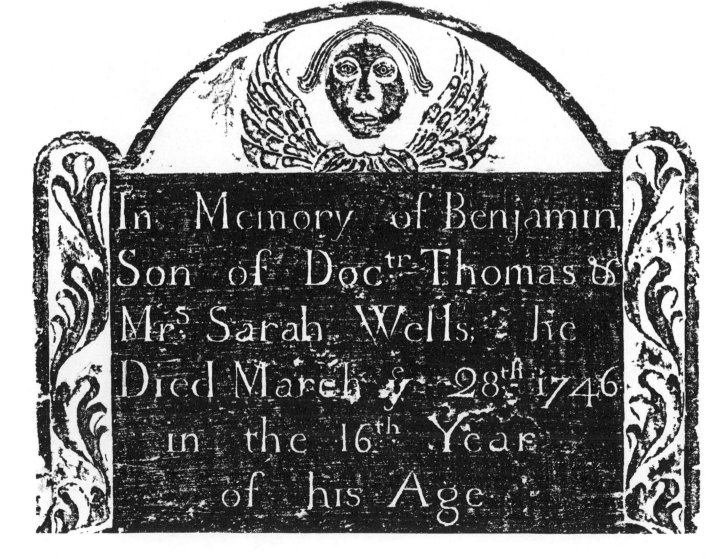

*Plate 43*

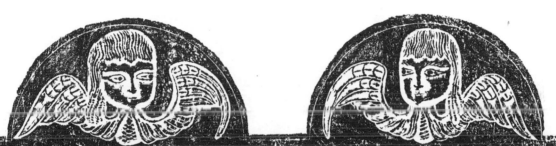

MARCIA GIBBS, Daught of Henry and Mercy Gibbs, died Nov. 17th 1791. Aged 4 Years & 2 Weeks

HENRY GIBBS eldest Son of Henry and Mercy Gibbs, died Dec. 14th 1791. Aged 8 Years & 7 Months.

*Infatiate Archer! could not one fuffice?*
*Thy fhaft flew twice, & twice my peace was flain,*
*And twice, ere twice yon moon had fill'd her horn.*

*Young*

*Plate 44*

*Plate 45*

Memento mori

ERECTED
IN memory of
Mrs Jennet Strongmun
Relict of
Mr Henry Strongmun
who died
Novr ye 20th 1792
In the 73d year
of her age.

*Plate 46*

*Plate 47*

Here Lyes Buried the Body of M.rs SARAH RICE, Wife of M.r NATHANIEL RICE, She Died Jan.y the 4.th Anno. Dom

IN MEMORY of M.r WILLIAM

*Plate 48*

In Memory of
M<sup>rs</sup> Hannah Eliot

My glaſs is run

ERECTED
In Memory of

*Plate 49*

*Plate* 50

Memento mori

Here lies buried the Body of Cap⸏ JOSEPH BARRETT Son of Deacon Humphry and

MEMORY OF M⸏ BENJAMIN HAWARD

*Plate 51*

*Plate* 52

Plate 53

*Plate 54*

Plate 55

Sacred to the memory of the
Rev NEHEMIAH RARKER,
first Pastore of the Church of
Christ in Hubbardston
Ordained to the Sacred office
June 13th 1770, and deceased
Aug 20th 1801, in the
60th Year of his age
much lamented
In him were unted the kind
Husband the tender and
indulgent Father, the
eloquent orator and
benevolent Christian

His hand while they his alms bestow'd,
A glorious future harvest Sow'd,

*Plate 56*

Plate 57

In Memory of
Mr CALEB Cooley son
of Mr CALEB & Mrs MARY
COOLEY
& Confort to
Mrs EXPERIENCE COOLEY

*Plate 58*

Plate 59

HEAR LIES Y REMAINS OF
Mrs SARAH HART WIFE
TO A Mr CONSTANT HART
WHO DIED MARCH Y
1752 IN Y 26

In Memory of Lieut
BENJAMIN GILBERT
who died June y 24th
AD 1760, in the 69

*Plate 60*

*Plate 61*

In Memory of
Mary the Wife of
Simeon Harvey
Who Departed this
Life December 20th
1785 In 39th year of
Her age on her left
Arm lieth the Infant
Which was still

*Plate 62*

*Plate 63*

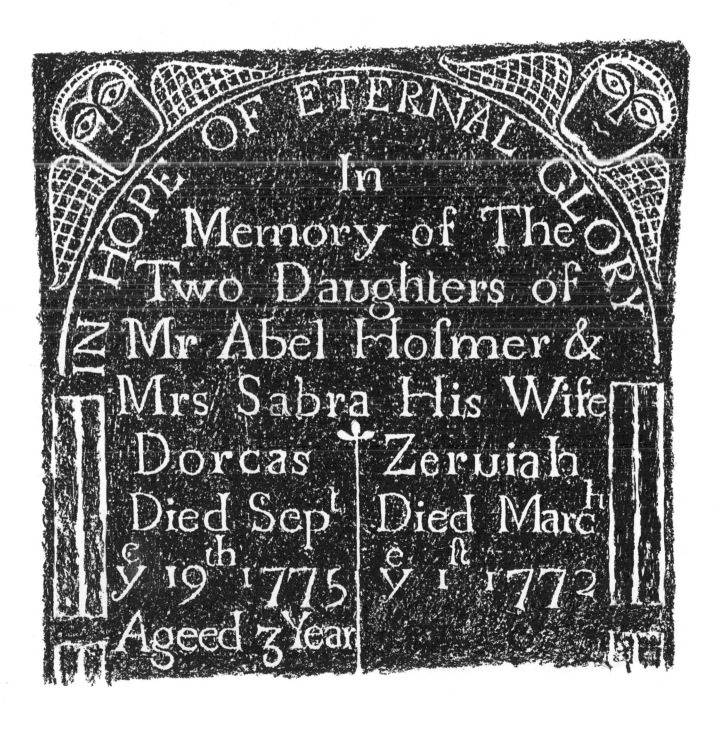

IN HOPE OF ETERNAL GLORY

In
Memory of The
Two Daughters of
Mr Abel Hofmer &
Mrs Sabra His Wife
Dorcas · Zeruiah
Died Sep<sup>t</sup> · Died Marc<sup>h</sup>
y<sup>e</sup> 19 1775 · y<sup>e</sup> 1 1772
Ageed 3 Year

*Plate 64*

In memory of Oliver
Bacon, Son of Lieuͭ Oliver
& Mrs Rebecca Bacon
who was killed by lightning
July 2ⁿᵈ 1801. aged
8 Years, & 7 months.

Plate 65

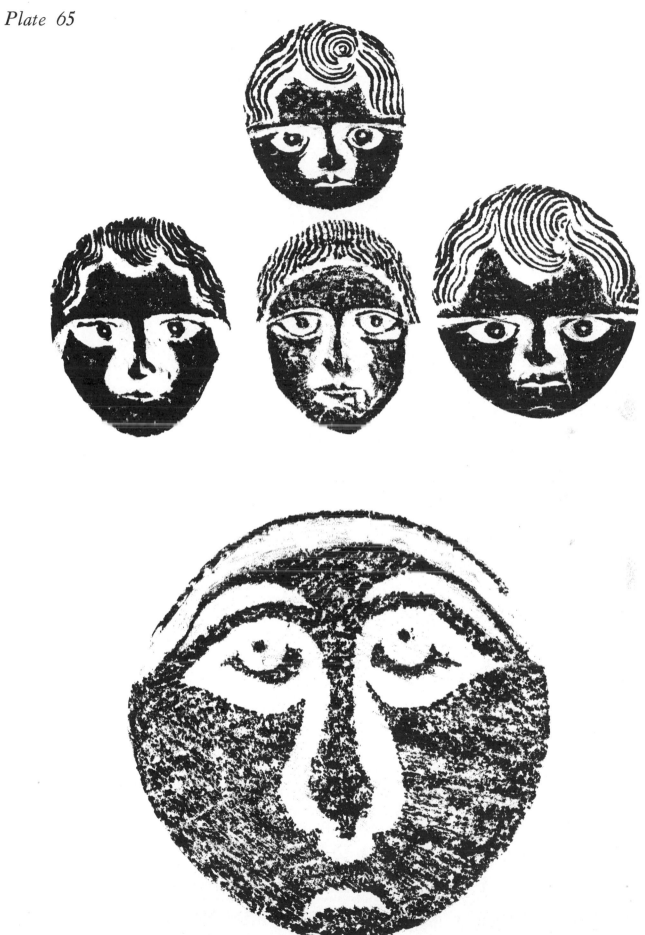

*Plate 66*

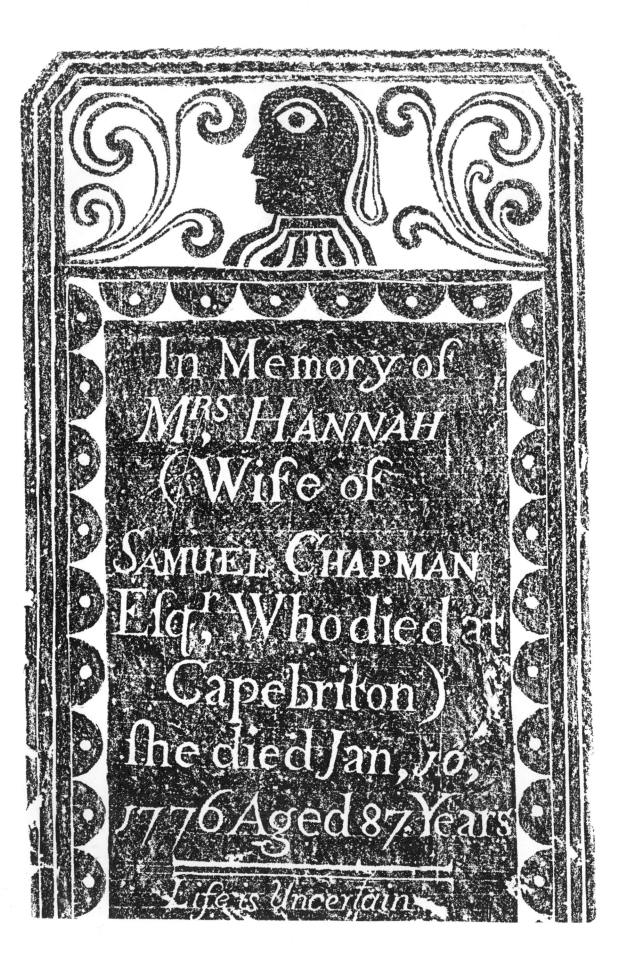

Plate 67

*Plate 68*

Plate 69

In memory of

Mrs SARAH WHEELER,

wife of

Mr Elisha Wheeler,

who died

Dec. 6 1775. Aged 21.

Within the confines of the tomb
Death lays my body low
Snatch'd from my friends in early bloom.

Plate 70

Plate 73

*Plate 74*

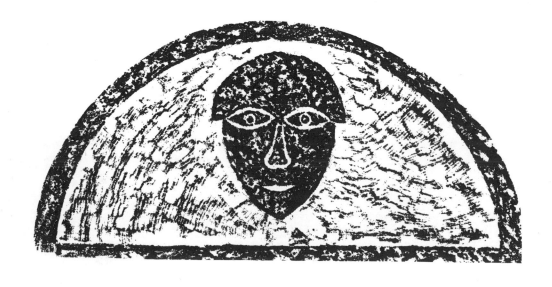

Willows & Urns

Plate 75

Plate 75

*Plate* 76

Plate 77

*Plate* 78

Plate 79

Oct. 3, 1788.

*Plate  80*

Plate 81

*Plate 82*

Here in the cold bed of
death, free from trouble and
pain, sleeps at rest, Eliza
Bradford, Daughter of
Fordyce & Elizabeth
Foster, who died *Oct. 14.*
1811. Æt. 14 Months

*Sleep on sweet child for God*
*our trust*
*Will raise thee blooming from*
*the dust.*

*Plate 83*

*Plate 84*

*Plate 85*

In Memory of
JAMES HULL ALLEN,
Son of Capt Gabriel &
Mrs. Sarah Allen:
He departed this Life the
6ᵗʰ of Auguſt, 1793. Aged
15 Years, 3 Months & 21 Days
Young Friends regard this ſolemn Truth,
Soon you may die like me in youth:
Death is a debt to nature dye,
Which I have paid, and ſo muſt you.

*Plate 86*

*Plate 87*

*Plate 88*

*Plate 89*

*Plate 90*

Plate 91

IN

Memory of

Mr Jacob Child.

who died

July 30. 1822

Æ. 76 years 3 mon.

& 6 days.

My soul! death swallows up thy
fears,
My grave-clothes wipe away all

*Plate 92*

Plate 93

Plate 94

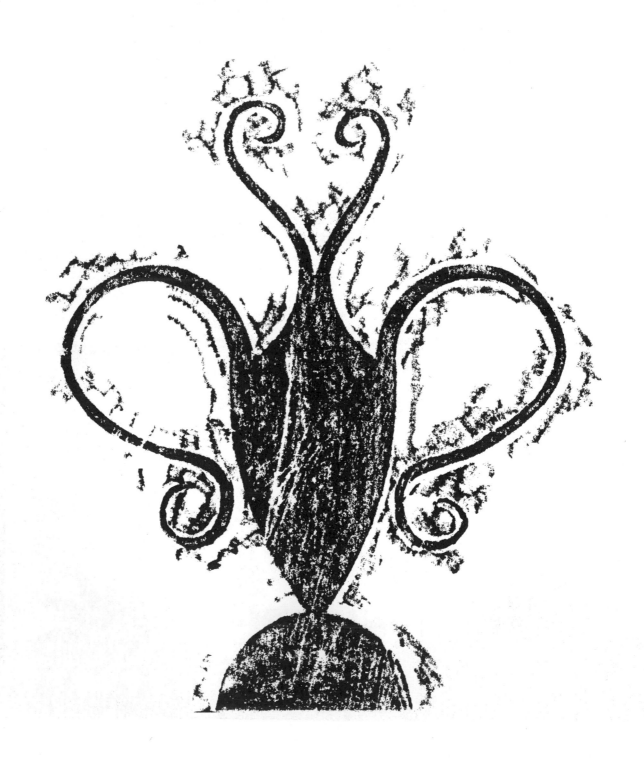

Plate 95

In Memory of
EDWIN STEARNS,
Son of Mr Jonas & Mrs.
Lydia Stearns,
who died
Aug. 6, 1814.
Æt 13.

*Plate 96*

Plate 97

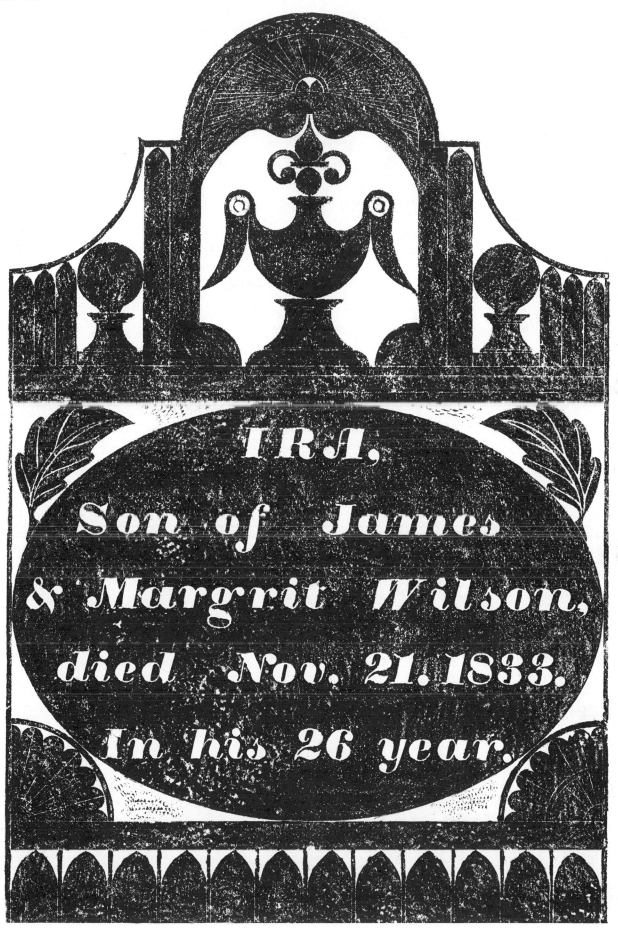

*Plate 98*

Plate 99

ERECTED BY
ALEX. LELAND,
In memory of his Wife
Margaret, Who died

July 10 1822, in

the 40th year of

her age.

Dear Children, Remember

That your Mother lies here.

*Plate 100*

*Plate 101*

*Plate* 102

Plate 103

Here Lies the Boddy of

Mrs Mary Wilder wife of John

Wilder she wos born the 6

of June 1781 and died Oct' 20

1809 in the 29 year of her age

How lov'd how valu'd once avails the not
To whom related or by whom begat
A heap of dust alone remains of thee
'Tis all thou art and what we all must be

*Plate 104*

Plate 105

Plate 106

Plate 107

*Plate 108*

*Plate 109*

WIDOW
ACHSAH STILES
relict of the late
Ebenezer Stiles,
died Jan. 30, 1842,
Æ. 69.

Adieu! my friends. my work is done,
And to the dust I must return.
Far hence, away, my spirit flies,
To find a home beyond the skies.

*Plate 110*

Plate 111

Plate 112

IN memory of
Deacon
ROBERT THOMPSON
who died
July 10th 1808
Ætatis LXXXIV.

God's own right hand his saints shall raise
From death's dark shade to sing his praise,
And bring them to the courts above,
To see his succeed in his love.

*Plate 113*

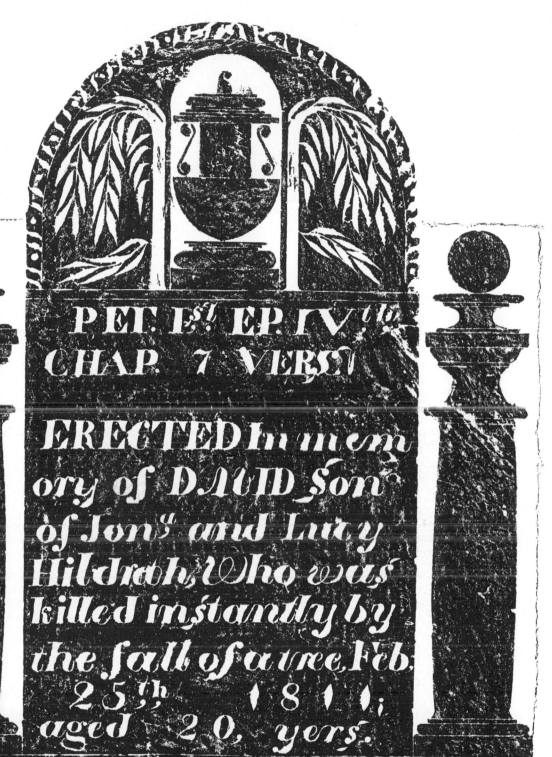

PET. E.<sup>st</sup> EP. IV<sup>th.</sup>
CHAP. 7 VERS.

ERECTED In mem
ory of DAUID Son
of Jon<sup>a</sup> and Lucy
Hildrah, Who was
killed instantly by
the fall of a tree, Feb.
25<sup>th</sup>   18    ;
aged  20, yers.

The grave is near the cradle seen,
How swift the moments pass between,
And whisper as they   fly,
Unthinkin man I remember this,
Thou midst thy sublunary bliss,
Must groan and gasp and die.

Plate 114

*Plate 115*

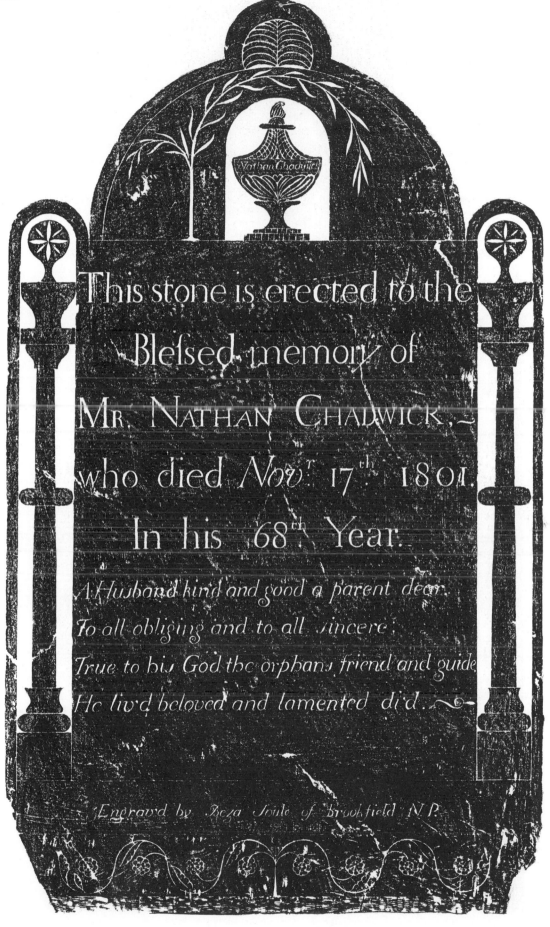

This stone is erected to the

Blefsed memory of

Mr. NATHAN CHADWICK,

who died Nov.r 17th 1801.

In his 68th Year.

A Husband kind and good a parent dear.
To all obliging and to all sincere;
True to his God the orphans friend and guide
He liv'd beloved and lamented di'd.

Engrav'd by Beza Soule of Brookfield N.P.

*Plate 116*

Plate 117

Remember Death

In memory of Mr. ROBERT RICH who died Sep<sup>t</sup> 27 1817. In his 41<sup>st</sup> year.

God is Just Supreme his power, Mortals be silent a<sup>nd</sup> adore.

*Plate 118*

*Plate 119*

*Plate 120*

Plate 121

*Plate 122*

*Plate 123*

*Plate 124*

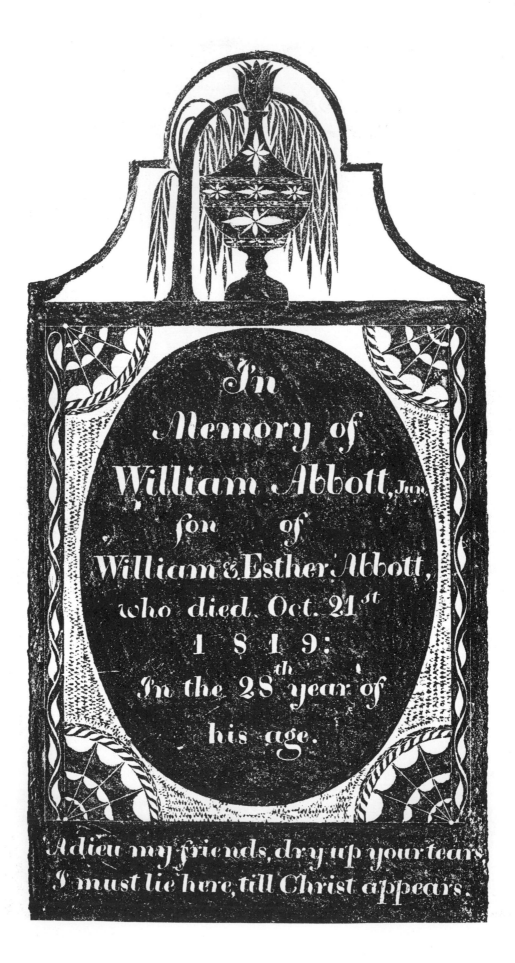

Decorative
Motifs,
Symbols
& Oddities

Plate  125

*Plate  126*

Plate 127

*Plate 128*

Eleazer Willson, son of
Mr. Ephraim & Mrs.
Sibbel Willson, died
15 July 1785; aged 1
year 11 months & 20
days.

Though I was young yet I must die,
And hasten to eternity.

Plate 129

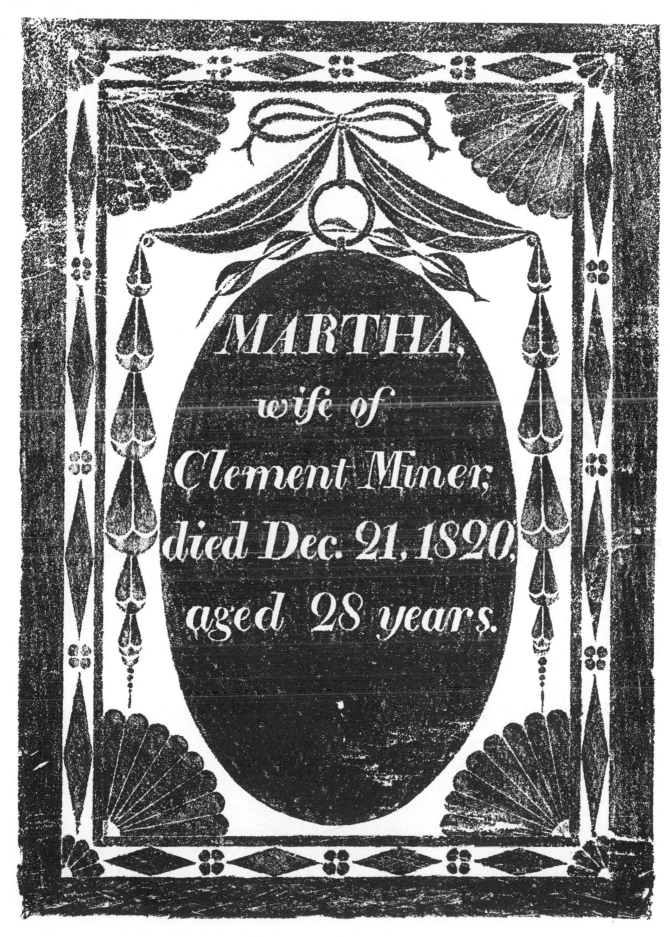

Plate 130

*Plate 131*

Here is entered the re-
mains of Isaac A. Spof-
ford, son of Dea". Eleaz.<sup>r</sup>
& Mrs. Mary Spofford,
a brand plucked from
the ashes of Rev. Laban
Ainsworth's house 13
Feb. 1788. Æ. 8.

Oh say grim Death, why thus destroy,
The parents hope, their fondest joy,
Cease man to ask the hidden cause
God wills tis done revere his laws

Plate 132

*Plate 133*

*Plate 134*

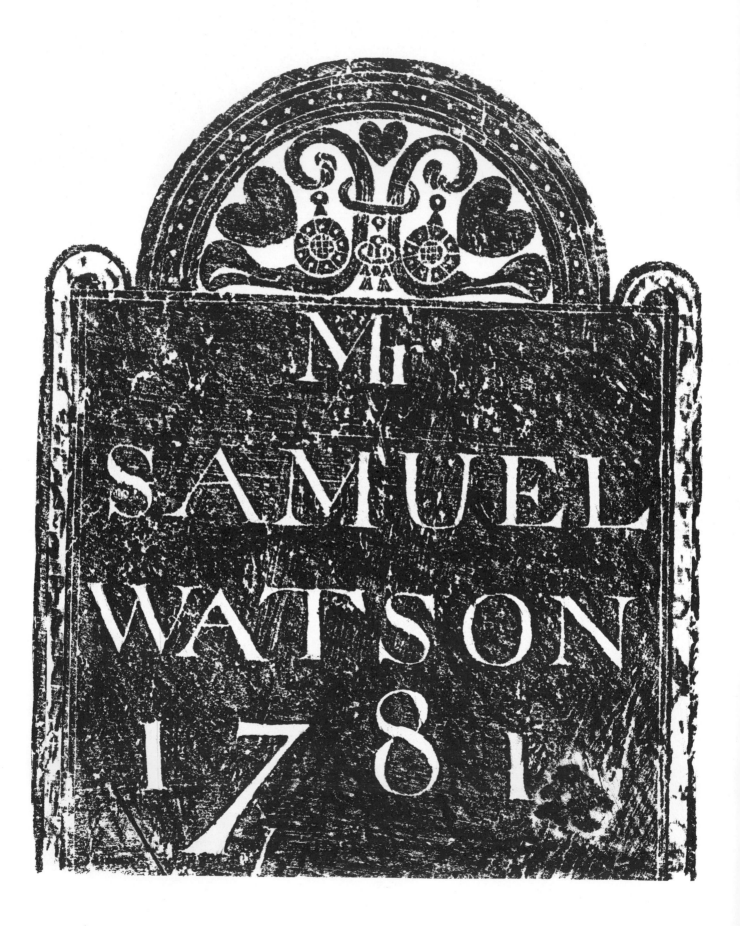

Plate 135

*Plate 136*

Oren son of
Kias & Polly
Allen, died 27
Aug. 1818, Æ. 2.

Plate 139

*Plate 140*

*Plate 141*

In Memory of,
JAMES GOULDING
Son of Mr John R &
Mrs Ruth Goulding,
who died
Sep 1 7 9 6
Æt. 5 years

*Plate  142*

Here lies the Body of
M<sup>rs</sup>. ABIGAIL PAINE,
Relict Widow of
M<sup>r</sup>. SAMUEL PAINE;
She Died Jan<sup>y</sup> y<sup>e</sup> 13<sup>th</sup>.
1752: in the 80<sup>th</sup>.
Year of Her Age.

Plate 143

Plate 144

*Plate 145*

In Memory of
Sophia Nurſe,
daugʳ. of Mr. Jonᵃ.
& Mrs. Ruth Nurse,
who died July 19ᵗʰ.
1795 in the 3ᵈ year
of her age.

*Plate 146*

Plate 147

*Plate 148*

Plate 149

Erected

In Memory of

Mrs Sibbel Howard wife of
Mr
Nathan Howard who

Plate 150

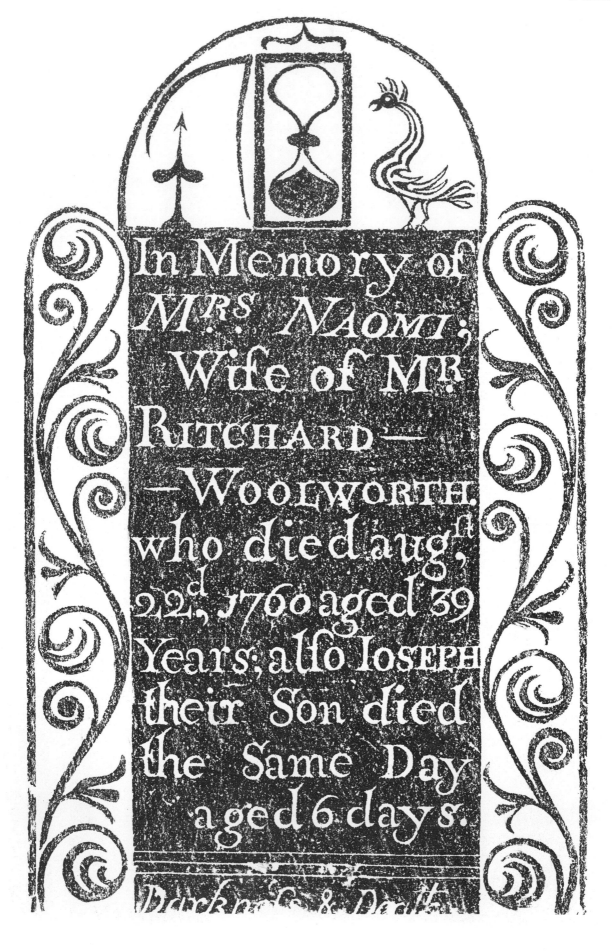

In Memory of
Mrs. NAOMI;
Wife of Mr.
RITCHARD—
—WOOLWORTH.
who die'd augst.
22d, 1760 aged 39
Years: also IOSEPH
their Son died
the Same Day
aged 6 days.

Darkness & Death

Plate 151

In Memory of Mr

OTHNIEL WILLIAMS

who died May 22, 1815,

in the 55 year of his age

*Plate 152*

Plate 153

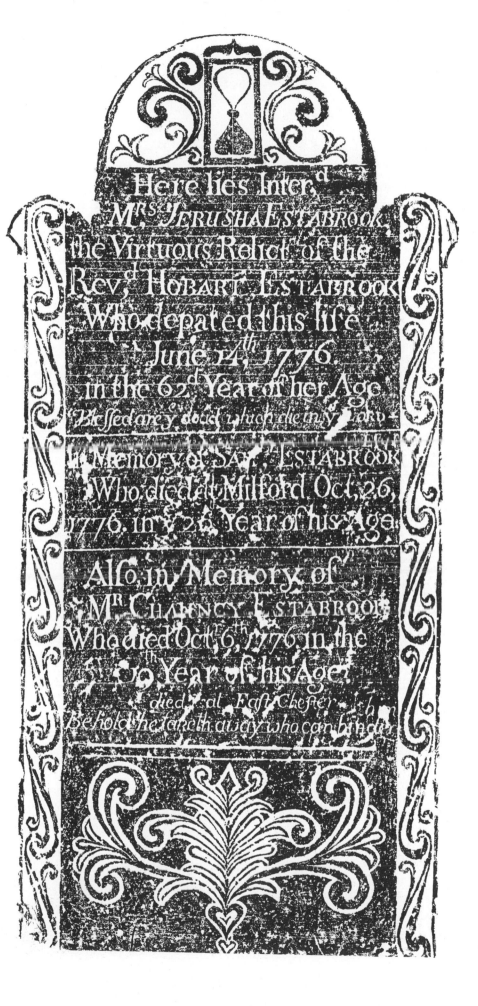

Here lies Inter.d
M.rs JERUSHA ESTABROOK,
the Virtuous Relict of the
Rev.d HOBART ESTABROOK
Who depated this life
June 14.th 1776
in the 62.d Year of her Age
Blessed are y.e dead which die in y.e Lord

In Memory of SAM.l ESTABROOK
Who died at Milford Oct, 26,
1776. in y.e 26 Year of his Age

Also in Memory of
M.r CHAUNCY ESTABROOK
Who died Oct. 6. 1776. in the
30 Year of his age.
died at East Chester
Behold he taketh away who can hinder

*Plate  154*

his  is  near          the  spot
that  the  Indians  Encamp'd  the
Night after they  took  Mr Johnson  &
Family  Mr Laberee  &  Farnsworth
August  30th  1754  And  Mrs
Johnson was  Deliver'd  of  her Child
Half a  mile  up      this  Brook

When  troubles  near  the  Lord  is  kind
He  hears  the  Captives  crys.
He  can  subdue  the  savage  mind,
And  Learn  it  sympathy.

Plate 155

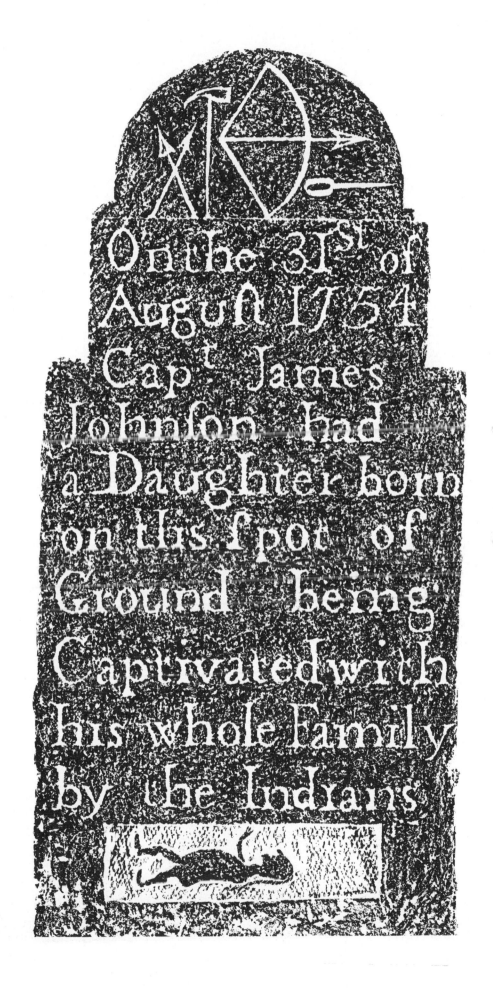

On the 31st of
August 1754
Capt James
Johnson had
a Daughter born
on this spot of
Ground being
Captivated with
his whole Family
by the Indians

*Plate 156*

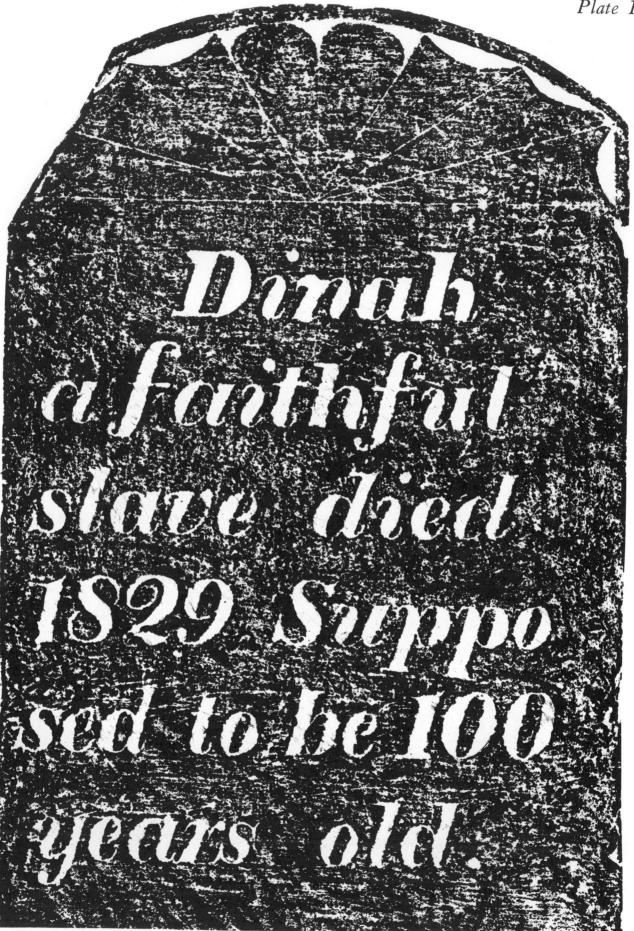

*Plate 157*

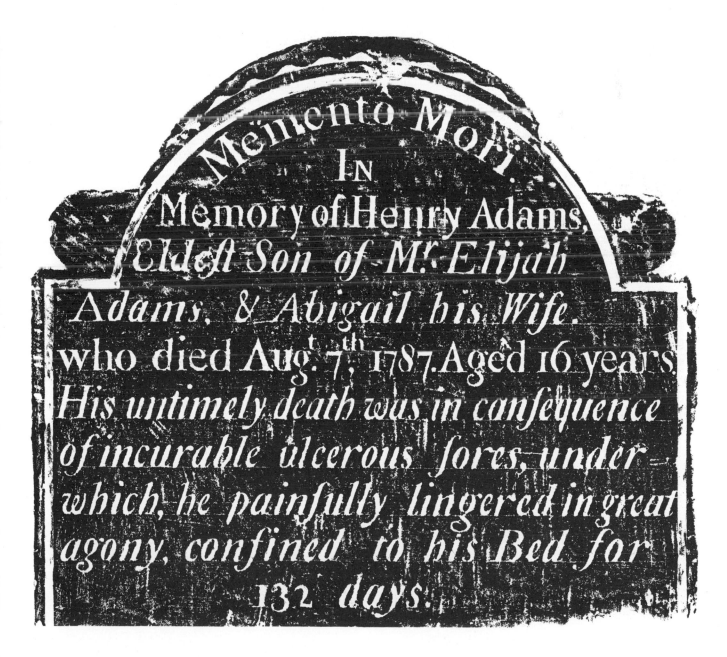

Memento Mori.

In
Memory of Henry Adams,
Eldest Son of Mr Elijah
Adams, & Abigail his Wife.
who died Augt. 7th. 1787. Aged 16 years.
His untimely death was in consequence
of incurable ulcerous sores, under
which, he painfully lingered in great
agony, confined to his Bed for
132 days.

*Plate 158*

*Photographs*

*Plate 159*

*Plate 160*

Plate 161

*Plate 162*

Plate 163

*Plate 164*

Plate 165

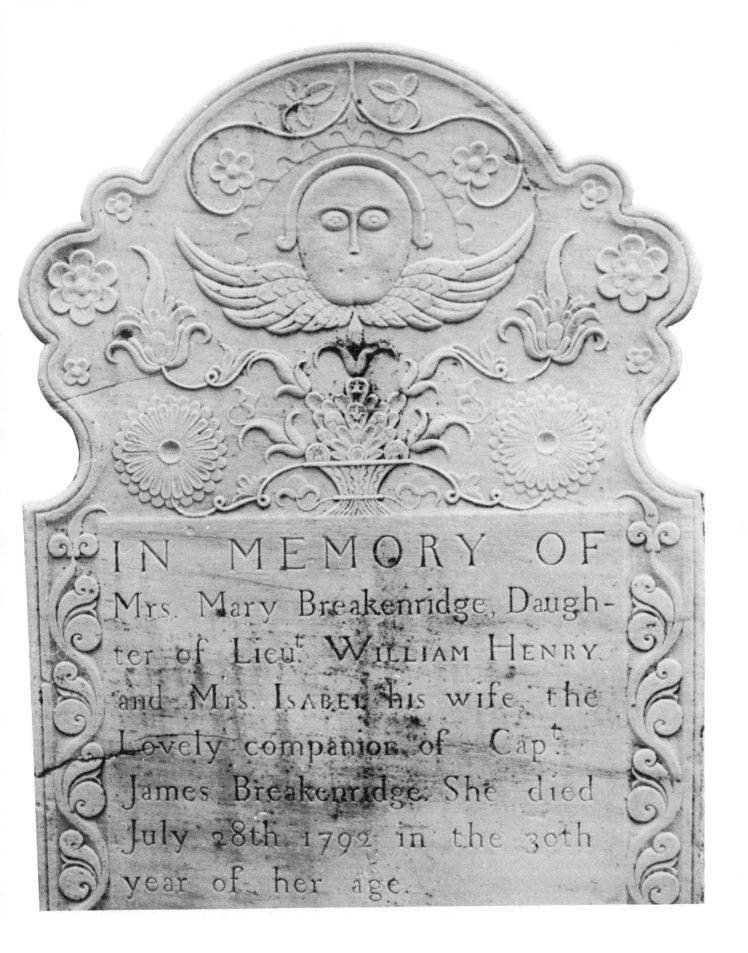

Plate 166

Plate 167

*Plate 168*

Plate 169

*Plate 170*

Plate 171

*Plate 172*

*Plate 173*

*Plate 174*

Plate 175

Plate 176

Plate 177

*Plate 178*

*Plate 183*

Plate 184

*Plate  185*

Plate 186

"An honest man's the noblest work of God."

CAPTAIN EPHRAIM CARTER
died May 19.1798 age 55.
He was a comfort & staff to aged
Parents, a guide to Children,
a faithful & affectionate Confort,
a Patron & Lover of Free Masonry,
& a constant Benefactor to the Poor.
Animated with public Spirit,
he promoted the good of society,
and in his numerous private and
public employments, acted with
strict integrity.
He was a sincere Christian & his

Plate  187

*Plate 188*

*Plate 189*

*Plate 190*

Plate 191

IN MEMORY OF
Mrs. HARRIET DAVIS,
WIFE OF
SIMON DAVIS Esq.
AND DAUGHTER OF
Mr. AMOS KETCHUM
OF THE CITY OF
NEW YORK,
WHO DIED AUGUST 16, A.D. 1828
IN THE 28, YEAR
OF HER AGE,

Plate 192

*Plate 193*

*Plate 194*

Plate 195

Life is Short.

In Memory of Mrs. ELISA
BETH, wife of Enſ WILLIAM
SPEAR ſhe died 1 June AD.
1799 in the 36 year of her
age.
Death is a debt to nature due,
Which I have paid, & ſo muſt you,
Weep not for me, dry up your te
   ars.
I muſt lye here, till Chriſt appears

# TABLE
# OF WIDTHS OF RUBBINGS

Virtually all the rubbings had to be reduced in order to fit into the format of this book. The following table gives the width in inches of the stones at their widest point.

PLATE 1. 25¼.
PLATE 2. 23½.
PLATE 3. top, 10¾; center, 12; bottom, 13¼.
PLATE 4. 18⅜.
PLATE 5. top, 20⅜; bottom, 18½.
PLATE 6. 15⅛.
PLATE 7. 17⅝.
PLATE 8. top, 13; center, 11¾; bottom, 17.
PLATE 9. top, 14¼; bottom, 18.
PLATE 10. top, 22½; bottom, 30⅛.
PLATE 11. 22⅛.
PLATE 12. top, 31; bottom, 23¼.
PLATE 13. 20¼.
PLATE 14. 35½.
PLATE 15. top, 19⅛; bottom, 16⅞.
PLATE 16. top, 19¼; bottom, 20¾.
PLATE 17. top, 18⅛; bottom, 14½.
PLATE 18. top, 17⅞; bottom, 20⅞.
PLATE 19. 25¼.
PLATE 20. top, 23⅝; bottom, 19⅞.
PLATE 21. 19⅛.
PLATE 22. 23¾.
PLATE 23. top, 17½; bottom, 23½.
PLATE 24. 22⅜.
PLATE 25. top, 26½; bottom, 19¾.
PLATE 26. 15.
PLATE 27. top, 18⅝, bottom, 20⅝.
PLATE 28. top, 19¼; bottom, 10¼.
PLATE 29. 17.
PLATE 30. 19.
PLATE 31. 14½.
PLATE 32. top, 14½; bottom, 16¼.
PLATE 33. 21⅛.
PLATE 34. 21⅜.
PLATE 35. top, 21; bottom, 16⅜.
PLATE 36. 19¾.
PLATE 37. 20¼.
PLATE 38. 20¾.
PLATE 39. top, 22⅞; bottom, 18⅛.
PLATE 40. top, 14⅛; bottom, 15⅝.
PLATE 41. 21.
PLATE 42. 16⅞.
PLATE 43. 22¾.
PLATE 44. 19½.
PLATE 45. 24.
PLATE 46. top, 30; bottom, 28¼.

PLATE 47. top, 30⅝; bottom, 22¼.
PLATE 48. top, 23¼; bottom, 30⅞.
PLATE 49. 36.
PLATE 50. top, 34⅜; bottom, 24¾.
PLATE 51. 20.
PLATE 52. 26⅞.
PLATE 53. 18¼.
PLATE 54. top, 3½, bottom, 17⅞.
PLATE 55. 34⅛.
PLATE 56. 17.
PLATE 57. top, 17⅝; bottom, 26¾.
PLATE 58. top, 23; bottom, 27½.
PLATE 59. top, 27½; bottom, 28½.
PLATE 60. 27.
PLATE 61. 19¼.
PLATE 62. top, 20⅝; bottom, 14.
PLATE 63. 28¼.
PLATE 64. 20.
PLATE 65. top, 2⅝; center left, 2⅞; center middle, 2⅝; center right, 3¼; bottom, 6⅞.
PLATE 66. 20⅜.
PLATE 67. 22¼.
PLATE 68. 24¼.
PLATE 69. 23½.
PLATE 70. top, 17¾; bottom, 21½.
PLATE 71. 21¾.
PLATE 72. 15.
PLATE 73. top, 16⅛; bottom, 16⅞.
PLATE 74. top, 2⅝; second, 8⅝; third, 7; bottom, 9¼.
PLATE 75. top, 21¾; bottom, 20½.
PLATE 76. 11⅜.
PLATE 77. top, 7¾; bottom, 14⅞.
PLATE 78. top, 6½; bottom, 12¾.
PLATE 79. 19.
PLATE 80. top, 12; bottom, 14¼.
PLATE 81. top. 15⅛; bottom, 15.
PLATE 82. 11¼.
PLATE 83. 26¾.
PLATE 84. top, 9½; bottom, 6⅝.
PLATE 85. 14¾.
PLATE 86. top, 22¼; bottom, 28.
PLATE 87. top, 24⅜; bottom, 29.
PLATE 88. 26¾.
PLATE 89. 17.
PLATE 90. top, 2⅞; bottom, 29¾.
PLATE 91. 28.
PLATE 92. top, 5⅛; bottom, 26.
PLATE 93. top, 9½; bottom, 16.
PLATE 94. 5¾.
PLATE 95. 16¼.
PLATE 96. 17¼.
PLATE 97. 22⅝.
PLATE 98. top, 20⅜; bottom, 20⅞.
PLATE 99. 22¾.
PLATE 100. 23⅞.
PLATE 101. 19.
PLATE 102. 15¼.
PLATE 103. 29⅞.
PLATE 104. 22¾.
PLATE 105. top, 23⅛; bottom, 23⅞.
PLATE 106. top, 15½; bottom, 23.
PLATE 107. top, 5⅛; bottom, 6⅛.
PLATE 108. top, 23¾; bottom, 21½.
PLATE 109. 21⅞.
PLATE 110. 21¾.
PLATE 111. top, 19¾; bottom, 22½.
PLATE 112. 30.
PLATE 113. 20¾.
PLATE 114. top, 3¼; bottom, 6⅞.
PLATE 115. 23.
PLATE 116. 27½.
PLATE 117. 31.
PLATE 118. 22.
PLATE 119. 17⅝.
PLATE 120. 21⅛.
PLATE 121. 14¼.
PLATE 122. 16.
PLATE 123. 23¾.
PLATE 124. 17⅝.
PLATE 125. top, 11⅞; center, 15½; bottom, 14⅞.
PLATE 126. 14⅛.
PLATE 127. 3⅛.
PLATE 128. 15¼.
PLATE 129. 22¾.
PLATE 130. left, 18½; center, 17½; right, 20⅞.
PLATE 131. 21¼.
PLATE 132. 3½.

PLATE 133. 21½.
PLATE 134. 13⅛.
PLATE 135. 8⅛.
PLATE 136. 11½.
PLATE 137. top, 12¼; bottom, 26.
PLATE 138. 52.
PLATE 139. 6.
PLATE 140. 18⅛.
PLATE 141. 17¾.
PLATE 142. 26.
PLATE 143. top, 23; bottom, 5.
PLATE 144. top, 20⅛; bottom, 38.
PLATE 145. 14.
PLATE 146. 3¼.
PLATE 147. top, 4⅜; second, 5; third, 7½; bottom, 8.
PLATE 148. 20¼.
PLATE 149. 19¾.
PLATE 150. 21⅛.
PLATE 151. 23⅞.
PLATE 152. 17.
PLATE 153. 23¼.
PLATE 154. 29.
PLATE 155. 16.
PLATE 156. 12⅜.
PLATE 157. top, 4⅛; bottom, 20¼.
PLATE 158. 54.

# NOTES ON THE PLATES

PLATE 1    Bolton, Mass. Typical geometric style of stone carving done by the Worcester family of Harvard, Mass. (see also plate 3 and 132). Simple scrollwork adorns the sides of the stone.

PLATE 2    Marblehead, Mass. This stone was designed by Henry Christian Geyer (d. c. 1793), a Boston stonecutter. The hourglass flanked by bones warns that time passes rapidly, an idea which is reinforced by the depiction of the scythe, the sun (note its anthropomorphic face) and the moon. The skeleton, with its laurel-wreathed head is a grim reminder of the victory of death, while the bats symbolize the evil of the world. These somber motifs are offset by the rope-like snake swallowing its tail, an expression of eternity, and the winged cherubs, whose innocence evokes the spirituality of life in the world to come. Acanthus leaves ornament the stone.

PLATE 3    Death's-heads, emblems of man's mortality, two of which are depicted with wings, probably symbolic of the flight of the soul. The head in the center design, with its simple geometric motifs, is unmistakably the work of a member of the Worcester family of Harvard, Mass. (see also plates 1 and 132).

PLATE 4    Less somber death's-head with wings and ornamental border work.

PLATE 5    Death's-heads with wings. The style of carving displayed on the stone at the top bears a great resemblance to the description of the work of a member of the Lamson family of Charlestown, Mass., possibly to Joseph Lamson (1658-1722), given by Harriette M. Forbes in her book, *Gravestones of Early New England* (Boston, 1927), pp. 41-2. This stone gives evidence of what was supposed to be Joseph Lamson's "characteristic death symbol"—the head has a broad top to it, while the eyebrows have curves ending in little hooks (see also plates 7, 10, top, and 12, top, for similarly carved heads).

PLATE 6    Hollow-eyed skull and crossbones with wings (see also plates 9, top, and 13).

PLATE 7    This somewhat compressed death's-head with wings may be the work of a member of the Lamson family of Charlestown (see also plates 5, 10, top, and 12, top; and note to plate 5).

PLATE 8  The two death's-heads in the designs at top and center have forked nostrils (see also plate 9, bottom). Bottom: Spencer, Mass. A skeleton in full view reclines in the detail at bottom.

PLATE 9  Death's-heads with wings. Note resemblance of design at top to plates 6 and 13; and design at bottom to plate 8, top and center.

PLATE 10  A winged death's-head and leafy motifs adorn the stone at top which may be the work of a member of the Lamson family of Charlestown (see also plates 5, 7, and 12, top; and note to plate 5). Bottom: Marblehead, Mass. (1757). This design is distinctive for its stark arrangement of symbols. It is also a rare example of a skull carved in profile. The hourglass, scythe, and crossbones are graphic symbols of mortality.

PLATE 11  East Woodstock, Conn. Death's-head with wings.

PLATE 12  A shell-like ornament is suspended above the skull in the stone at top which may be the work of a member of the Lamson family of Charlestown (see also plates 5, 7, and 10, top; and note to plate 5). The curly-headed angel with wings in the bottom design is close to portraiture in the expressive down lines around the mouth. The head is flanked by crudely incised flowers.

PLATE 13  Death's-head with wings (see also plates 6 and 9, top).

PLATE 14  Oxford, N. H. The anonymous cutter of the stone has been called the "Hook and Eye man" (see Forbes, *op. cit.*, pp. 101-2) from his way of carving noses and eyes. Other evidences of his work are to be found in the Connecticut Valley. The crown adorning the skull is probably intended as a symbol of the soul's victory over death.

PLATE 15  Angels' heads. The head in the top design with its smooth hair is close to portraiture (see also plate 69), while the head in the stone at bottom (1778) is much more stylized.

PLATE 16  Angels' heads.

PLATE 17  Angels' heads executed with naive facial details in the outlines of the geometric style. The stone in the top design is dated 1796.

PLATE 18  Angels' heads. Top: Wales, Mass. (1791.) A crown adorns the head (see also plate 32, bottom). Bottom: East Woodstock, Conn.

PLATE 19  Canterbury, Conn. Square-jowled face with rope-like hair (see also plate 63) and pastoral collar representing the vocation of the deceased. The ornamental grapevines bordering the stone symbolize the rewards of Heaven and are also an emblem of Christ.

PLATE 20  Angels' heads. The head in the top design is dated 1824. The head at bottom, dated 1756, is surrounded by a nimbus.

PLATE 21  Angel's head.

PLATE 22  Sturbridge, Mass. (1778). Angel's head adorned with crown (see also plates 25, top, and 52). Note elaborate scrollwork and eight-pointed star, perhaps a Masonic symbol of nature's obedience to God.

PLATE 23  The head at top is unusual for its tightly coiled outline of hair. Bottom: Woodstock, Conn. Angel's head with crudely incised facial details.

PLATE 24  Woodstock, Conn. Implish-looking angel's head.

PLATE 25  Angels' heads. The square stone at top is similar in execution to that of plate 22 (see also plate 52 for a similarly styled head). The angel's head at bottom resembles that of plate 30.

PLATE 26  Angel's head out of which is growing an oak leaf, perhaps intended as a symbol of the strength of faith.

PLATE 27   Angels' heads. Note leaf arrangement in stone at top. Bottom: East Wood-stock, Conn. (1775).

PLATE 28   Angels' heads. Top: Salem, Mass. (1773). A single asphodel, traditionally a symbol of death, is incised on the stone at bottom.

PLATE 29   Angels' heads mark the burial place of two brothers.

PLATE 30   Angel's head (see also plate 25, bottom).

PLATE 31   Angel's head with crudely incised flowers.

PLATE 32   The naively detailed angel's head at top is an example of the geometric style of carving. Bottom: Wales, Mass. This design is adorned with a crown (see plate 18, top, for a similar crown design) and initials of the deceased. Note the cleft chin and abstract simplicity of the wings.

PLATE 33   Head with fan-shaped wings above which is an ivy vine, perhaps intended as a symbol of immortality.

PLATE 34   Unusually stylized figure, dated 1754, with distinctive wings. The border is a composite arrangement of floral motifs (see also plate 44).

PLATE 35   Angels' heads, one more skeletal, the other more cherubic. The head in the top design is distinctive for its pompadour hair and unfeathered wings. The stone at bottom may be the work of Captain John Bull (1734-1808) of Newport, Rhode Island (see Forbes, *op. cit.*, p. 97).

PLATE 36   Angel's head. A thistle emerges from the scroll relief at the base of the stone.

PLATE 37   Sturbridge, Mass. Curly-locked angel's head. The crudely incised grape-vine border is a traditional symbol of Christ and of the fruits of Heaven.

PLATE 38   Death's head with wings above which is either a palm, symbolizing the soul's victory over death, or an oak leaf.

PLATE 39   Angels' heads executed in the geometric style. The stone at top is dated 1795. An unfeathered wing arrangement is at bottom.

PLATE 40   Elongated angels' heads with curiously flattened jowls. The stone at bottom is dated 1768.

PLATE 41   Provincetown, Mass. Above this angel's head, which is close to portraiture, are mourning drapes.

PLATE 42   Angel's head.

PLATE 43   Angels' heads, both of which are close to portraiture.

PLATE 44   South Worthington, Mass. Unusually stylized head with odd wings (see also plate 179, bottom, and plate 34).

PLATE 45   Angel's head. The words "Memento mori" are inscribed on an ornamental ribbon. This headstone is distinctive for its pillared arch construction with simple Tuscan columns, an example of the influence of architectural motifs of the Federal period upon mortuary sculpture.

PLATE 46   Top and bottom: Bennington, Vt. The stone at top (1788) displays a pro-fusion of floral motifs, symbolic of the rewards of Heaven, dominated by an angel's head (see also plates 165 and 170). The bottom tablet, some-what less ornate, shows two angels' heads. This stone is decorated with ferns and asphodels. Two hearts with crosses inscribed within are at its base.

PLATE 47   An angel's head is shown at top. This stone is ornamented with an acanthus scroll border. At bottom (1708) is a portrait flanked by a scythe and hour-glass. Scrollwork borders the stone.

PLATE 48   At top is an angel's head mounted on a pedestal. The bottom design shows an angel's head atop a pedestal flanked by two funereal urns. An hourglass is centered between ceremonial ribbons on which the words "My glass is run" are inscribed.

PLATE 49   Angel's head.

PLATE 50    Top: Concord, Mass. Interesting use of scroll pediment into which a skull and crossbones and two portraits are incised. This architectural treatment is reminiscent of the more elaborate doorways of the Connecticut River Valley. Note the fluted columns with their composite capitals. Bottom: Warren, Mass. In the distinctive way in which the figure is carved—the low forehead, the long nose formed by continuing the eyebrows down, the straight-lined mouth, the unusually rounded shoulders with small neck— and the characteristic crossing of the *A's* in the inscription, this stone appears to be the work of William Young (1711-1795), the "thistle-carver of Tatnuck" (see Forbes, *op. cit.*, p. 83). (See also plates 57, top, 58, top, 62 top, and 169.)

PLATE 51    Moon-faced head of young girl garlanded with ribbons.

PLATE 52    Head adorned with crown and flanked by coiled wings (see also plates 22 and 25, top). This stone is distinctive for its geometric simplicity.

PLATE 53    Sturbridge, Mass. (1780). Portrait of wife of town's first settler. Head adorned with crown amid scrollwork.

PLATE 54    The head in the top design is enclosed in a circle which is possibly intended as a nimbus. Bottom: Uxbridge, Mass.

PLATE 55    Hubbardston, Mass. An attempt to represent the pastoral vocation of the deceased. Figure standing before a lectern beneath an archway. A rudimentary willow tree is bent ceremoniously over the figure. Stately Tuscan columns support the pediment.

PLATE 56    Wales, Mass. Portrait of youth whose death was the result of falling into a well. Crudely carved cypress trees, traditional symbols of death, adorn the stone.

PLATE 57    Forbes (op. cit., p. 83) describes one stone by William Young of Tatnuck as bearing a three-storied adaptation of the thistle. The stone at top is similar in many respects to the one reproduced by Mrs. Forbes and may very well be an example of his work (see also plates 50, bottom, 58, top, 62, top, 169; and notes to plate 50). Bottom: Wilbraham, Mass. (1785). Two portraits in profile between which is an hourglass adorned with a crown (see also plates 66 and 68).

PLATE 58    The stone at top may also be the work of William Young (see plates 50, bottom, 57, top, 62, top, 169; and notes to plates 50 and 57). At bottom is a head above a sun flanked by two cypress trees. The sun may represent either the end of life (in which case it would be setting) or the resurrection of the soul after death (in which case it would be rising). Note the supporting columns at the sides, typical of construction during the Federal period.

PLATE 59    At top is a head with pigtails. Bottom: North Brookfield, Mass. A graphic portrayal of death by the use of the full skeleton and open coffin with body in it. Vines decorate the borders of the stone.

PLATE 60    (1796). Columns support an arch, typical of Federal period construction, on which are arranged funereal urns and adaptations of a willow tree. The flames rising from the urns are emblems of the soul rising from its mortal ashes.

PLATE 61    Deerfield, Mass. Mother and infant in coffin.

PLATE 62    The stone at top (1752) bears the typical characteristics of the work of William Young of Tatnuck (see also plates 50, bottom, 57, top, 58, top, and 169; and notes to plate 50). Bottom: Crudely executed head in the geometric style.

PLATE 63    Woodstock, Conn. Square-jowled angels' heads (see also plate 19).

PLATE 64    Jaffrey, N. H. Figure niched beneath willow tree.

PLATE 65 A collection of heads from various stones with some attempts at portraiture.

PLATE 66 Longmeadow, Mass. Profile portrait amid scrollwork somewhat similar in execution to plates 57, bottom, and 68.

PLATE 67 Cameo portrait surrounded by geometric designs.

PLATE 68 West Woodstock, Conn. Profile portrait amid scrollwork (see also plates 57, bottom, and 66).

PLATE 69 Head amid leaf arrangement (see also plate 15, top). Note the funereal urns at the base of the stone out of which grow vines.

PLATE 70 At top (1797) is a naively detailed angel's head whose eyes are dreamily directed upwards to the motto "Death Overcomes All." Bottom: Paxton, Mass. (1769). Portrait of a Congregational minister before a lectern adorned with ceremonial tassels.

PLATE 71 Addison, Vt. Head above which are mourning drapes. The fan-shaped patterns on this stone were popular motifs in mortuary art. The two webbed designs flanking the head resemble bats' wings, while the details beneath look like suns.

PLATE 72 Niched figure with nimbus amid scrollwork.

PLATE 73 An angel's head is shown in the design at top. Bottom: Canterbury, Conn. (1775). Three curly-headed faces, a crown, and two fan-shaped designs adorn this stone. This pediment is similar to one of the two sons of John Trumbull (1794) reproduced by Forbes (*op. cit.*, p. 108) and attributed to the hand of John Walden (d. 1807) of Windham, Conn., whose work shows the stylistic influence of the Manning family of Connecticut.

PLATE 74 A collection of similarly carved heads. The middle one is flanked by two trees.

PLATE 75 The willow tree and urn became popular motifs of mortuary sculpture at the turn of the nineteenth century, and were evidence of an increasing tendency toward sentimentalization in gravestone art of that century. Urns, of course, were also fashionable accessories to buildings of the Federal period. In the design at top the willow signifies mourning and death. Two suns represent the resurrection of the soul after death.

PLATE 76 Woman leaning on urn weeping. This is typical of watercolor and embroidered mourning scenes so commonly executed by female seminary students during the Federal period. A chain of geometric designs decorates the base of the stone.

PLATE 77 The single flower within the urn seen at top bears resemblance to a rose with the possible significance that the soul attains its most perfect state after death. Note the checkered pattern of the urn at bottom.

PLATE 78 Conventionalized designs of willows and urn.

PLATE 79 Willow and urn resting on a brick tomb which in turn is supported by arch construction.

PLATE 80 Fan-shaped patterns in the design at top (1819) flank conventional representations of a willow and urn. Ornamental border work is at bottom.

PLATE 81 Funereal urns flanked by willow trees. Note the flame which rises from the urn at bottom (see note to plate 60).

PLATE 82 Westport, Conn. The initials of the deceased girl are carved on the urn.

PLATE 83 Ware Center, Mass. A willow and urn stand beneath an arch into which stylized willow branches appear to be carved. The checkered pattern of the keystone may have Masonic significance as a symbol of the variegated moments of pleasure and pain, prosperity and adversity in human life. Elaborate construction of the tombstone is typical of the Federal period. Note signature of stonecutter—"Martin Woods" of "Whately"—at base of stone. This practice of signing stones might prove to have been more common if it were possible to see that part of the stone which has sunk into the earth over the years (see, for example, plate 115). (There have been several stones unearthed near Hampton, Conn. which reveal the prices paid for them, another practice that might have been common.)

PLATE 105   Top: East Washington, N. H. (1836). Two stars, beneath which are fan-shaped patterns, flank a conventionally depicted urn. At bottom, a stylized willow tree and two somber obelisks are arranged in a tryptich effect.

PLATE 106   Bottom: East Washington, N. H. The urn is framed by a Gothic arch.

PLATE 107   Conventionalized designs of urns.

PLATE 108   Top: New Ipswich, N. H. (1820). Urn base is executed in floral design (for a similarly designed pediment see plate 116). Bottom: Hillsboro, N. H. (1840). Giant leaves flank the urn (see also plate 98, bottom).

PLATE 109   Hillsboro, N. H. Note leaves emanating from urn and stars just above.

PLATE 110   East Washington, N. H. (1840). A panel effect is created by geometric designs and urn.

PLATE 111   Stylized willow trees. Bottom: West Woodstock, Conn. (1805).

PLATE 112   Sharon, N. H. Construction of stone typical of Federal period. The swag ornaments on this slab are also found on the panels of fireplace mantels during this period.

PLATE 113   Another example of mortuary design during the Federal period.

PLATE 114   Conventionally executed urns.

PLATE 115   Warren, Mass. The stone was carved by Beza Soule (1750-1835) of Brookfield, Mass. Soule came from a family of stonecutters who did much work in the Worcester county of Massachusetts.

PLATE 116   Jaffrey, N. H. Note elaborate leaf ornamentation which contrasts with the solemnity of the willow and urn (see also plate 108, top, for a similarly executed pediment).

PLATE 117   Two rosettes flank the urn. Fan-shaped motifs are at the base of the stone.

PLATE 118   Provincetown, Mass. Obelisk-shaped stone with urn and willow.

PLATE 119   Conventionally executed willow and urn.

PLATE 120   A brick wall supports the traditional willow and urn in a cameo design which in turn is set upon scrollwork.

PLATE 121   The willow drapes a body encased in a coffin.

PLATE 122   Conventionally executed willow tree.

PLATE 123   The willow and urn are supported by elaborate pillared arch construction.

PLATE 124   Fan-shaped motifs prominently adorn this stone. Note the flames emanating from the urn (see note to plate 60).

PLATE 125   Details from various stones. The center design is similar to incised geometric motifs found on early blanket chests.

PLATE 126   Footstone with geometric decorations. This slab is unusual in that it lacks a date.

PLATE 127   Detail of a column supporting the all-seeing eye, a Masonic symbol.

PLATE 128   An abstract representation of a sunburst, probably symbolic of the soul's resurrection.

PLATE 129   Ceremonial drapes gaudily adorn this stone. Note the fan-shaped designs in the corners.

PLATE 130   Details of ornamental borders.

PLATE 131   Jaffrey, N. H. Interesting for its elongated finial motifs and the stately tassel suspended from the center of the arched top of the stone. The tassel is a motif commonly found in this southern area of New Hampshire (see also plate 158).

PLATE 132   This most extreme refinement of the geometrically styled head is another example of work done by a member of the Worcester family of Harvard, Mass. (see also plates 1 and 3).

PLATE 133   Uxbridge, Mass. (See plate 137, bottom.)

PLATE 134   A footstone on which heart-shaped designs are carved.

PLATE 159    Crudely executed angel's head.

PLATE 160    Salem, Mass. Angel's head.

PLATE 161    Thompson, Conn. Angel's head. The grapevine border at the sides brings to mind the parable of the vineyards.

PLATE 162    Sharon, N. H. This head is a realistic attempt at colonial portraiture (see also plate 168).

PLATE 163    Foster, R. I. Stylized angel's head (see also plate 175, bottom).

PLATE 164    Boston, Mass. Stone shows an attempt at colonial portraiture.

PLATE 165    Bennington, Vt. Stylized angel's head surrounded by a profusion of floral motifs (see also plates 46, top, and 170).

PLATE 166    Top: Hampton, Conn. Crude but realistic portrait of a woman in colonial cap and dress. Bottom: Two finials flank an hourglass above which is carved a head (see also plate 179).

PLATE 167    Bolton, Mass. A realistic attempt at portraiture and execution of colonial dress.

PLATE 168    North Sudbury, Mass. Four urns with flames emanating from two of them (see note to plate 60) flank a portrait (see plate 162).

PLATE 169    Sutton, Mass. This broad-shouldered figure may be the work of William Young, the "thistle-carver of Tatnuck" (see also plates 50, bottom, 57, top, 58, top, and top plate 50). Forbes (*op. cit.*, p. 83) notes that on Young's stones male figures were depicted by a conventional representation of a wig.

PLATE 170    Bennington, Vt. Angel's head dominated by luxurious floral motifs (see also plates 46, top, and 165).

PLATE 171    Canterbury, Conn. Geometrically executed head with almond-shaped eyes.

PLATE 172    Mendon, Mass. Stern-looking portrait.

PLATE 173    Union, Conn. Moon-shaped head with wings amid geometric motifs.

PLATE 174    Top: Boston, Mass. Cherubic angel's head. Bottom: Woodstock, Conn. Stylized angel's head.

PLATE 175    Top: Boston, Mass. A crown, intended either as an emblem of deity or as a symbol of the victory of the soul over death, is flanked by two cherubic angels' heads. Bottom: Foster, R. I. Impassive-looking angel's head (see also plate 163, bottom).

PLATE 176    Boston, Mass. A realistic attempt at colonial portraiture.

PLATE 177    Crudely executed angels' heads.

PLATE 178    Thompson, Conn. Head flanked by geometric motifs and vine border.

PLATE 179    Top: Two finial projections frame a portrait (see also plate 166, bottom). Bottom: South Worthington, Mass. Unusually stylized head with odd wings (see also plate 44).

PLATE 180    Top: Stylized angel's head. Bottom: Boston, Mass. Note the two-headed profile portraiture and the eight-pointed stars.

PLATE 181    Boston, Mass. Unusual full figure portrayal of Father Time.

PLATE 182    Floral motifs dominated by angel's head.

PLATE 183    Funereal urn surrounded by branch motif.

PLATE 184    Boston, Mass. In addition to the familiar pick and shovel, coffin and crossbones, tree and sun, a profusion of Masonic symbols dominates this stone (for an explanation, see note to plate 151). The crescent, along with the stars, is symbolic of nature's obedience to God.

PLATE 185    Twin trees in mortuary sculpture were meant to represent the so-called marriage trees which were often planted to flank the entrance of the newlyweds' residence. In this instance, the fallen tree symbolizes the death of the wife (see also plate 188).

Dover Books on Art

*PINE FURNITURE OF EARLY NEW ENGLAND, R. H. Kettell.* Over 400 illustrations, over 50 working drawings of early New England chairs, benches, beds, cupboards, mirrors, shelves, tables, other furniture esteemed for simple beauty and character. "Rich store of illustrations . . . emphasizes the individuality and varied design," ANTIQUES. 413 illustrations, 55 working drawings. 475pp. 8 x 10¾. T145 Clothbound $10.00

*BASIC BOOKBINDING, A. W. Lewis.* Enables both beginners and experts to rebind old books or bind paperbacks in hard covers. Treats materials, tools; gives step-by-step instruction in how to collate a book, sew it, back it, make boards, etc. 261 illus. Appendices. 155pp. 5⅜ x 8. T169 Paperbound $1.45

*DESIGN MOTIFS OF ANCIENT MEXICO, J. Enciso.* Nearly 90% of these 766 superb designs from Aztec, Olmec, Totonac, Maya, and Toltec origins are unobtainable elsewhere. Contains plumed serpents, wind gods, animals, demons, dancers, monsters, etc. Excellent applied design source. Originally $17.50. 766 illustrations, thousands of motifs. 192pp. 6⅛ x 9¼. T84 Paperbound $1.85

*A DIDEROT PICTORIAL ENCYCLOPEDIA OF TRADES AND INDUSTRY.* Manufacturing and the Technical Arts in Plates Selected from "L'Encyclopédie ou Dictionnaire Raisonné des Sciences, des Arts, et des Métiers," of Denis Diderot, edited with text by C. Gillispie. Over 2000 illustrations on 485 full-page plates. Magnificent 18th-century engravings of men, women, and children working at such trades as milling flour, cheesemaking, charcoal burning, mining, silverplating, shoeing horses, making fine glass, printing, hundreds more, showing details of machinery, different steps in sequence, etc. A remarkable art work, but also the largest collection of working figures in print, copyright-free, for art directors, designers, etc. Two vols. 920pp. 9 x 12. Heavy library cloth. T421 Two volume set $18.50

*SILK SCREEN TECHNIQUES, J. Biegeleisen, M. Cohn.* A practical step-by-step home course in one of the most versatile, least expensive graphic arts processes. How to build an inexpensive silk screen, prepare stencils, print, achieve special textures, use color, etc. Every step explained, diagrammed. 149 illustrations, 201pp. 6⅛ x 9¼. T433 Paperbound $1.55

*STICKS AND STONES, Lewis Mumford.* An examination of forces influencing American architecture: the medieval tradition in early New England, the classical influence in Jefferson's time, the Brown Decades, the imperial facade, the machine age, etc. "A truly remarkable book," SAT. REV. OF LITERATURE. 2nd revised edition. 21 illus. xvii + 240pp. 5⅜ x 8. T202 Paperbound $1.65

*THE AUTOBIOGRAPHY OF AN IDEA, Louis Sullivan.* The architect whom Frank Lloyd Wright called "the master," records the development of the theories that revolutionized America's skyline. 34 full-page plates of Sullivan's finest work. New introduction by R. M. Line. xiv + 335pp. 5⅜ x 8. T281 Paperbound $2.00

*ANIMALS IN MOTION, Eadweard Muybridge.* The largest collection of animal action photos in print. 34 different animals (horses, mules, oxen, goats, camels, pigs, cats, lions, gnus, deer, monkeys, eagles—and 22 others) in 132 characteristic actions. All 3919 photographs are taken in series at speeds up to 1/1600th of a second, offering artists, biologists, cartoonists a remarkable opportunity to see exactly how an ostrich's head bobs when running, how a lion puts his foot down, how an elephant's knee bends, how a bird flaps his wings, thousands of other hard-to-catch details. "A really marvellous series of plates," NATURE. 380 full-page plates. Heavy glossy stock, reinforced binding with headbands. 7⅞ x 10¾. T203 Clothbound $10.00

*THE BOOK OF SIGNS, R. Koch.* 493 symbols—crosses, monograms, astrological, biological symbols, runes, etc.—from ancient manuscripts, cathedrals, coins, catacombs, pottery. May be reproduced permission-free. 493 illustrations by Fritz Kredel. 104pp. 6⅛ x 9¼. T162 Paperbound $1.00

*A HANDBOOK OF EARLY ADVERTISING ART, C. P. Hornung.* The largest collection of copyright-free early advertising art ever compiled. Vol. I: 2,000 illustrations of animals, old automobiles, buildings, allegorical figures, fire engines, Indians, ships, trains, more than 33 other categories! Vol. II: Over 4,000 typographical specimens; 600 Roman, Gothic, Barnum, Old English faces; 630 ornamental type faces; hundreds of scrolls, initials, flourishes, etc. "A remarkable collection," PRINTERS' INK.
Vol. I: Pictorial Volume. Over 2000 illustrations. 256pp. 9 x 12.
T122 Clothbound $10.00
Vol. II: Typographical Volume. Over 4000 specimens. 319pp.
9 x 12. T123 Clothbound $10.00
Two volume set, Clothbound, only $18.50

*THE UNIVERSAL PENMAN, George Bickham.* Exact reproduction of beautiful 18th-century book of handwriting. 22 complete alphabets in finest English roundhand, other scripts, over 2000 elaborate flourishes, 122 calligraphic illustrations, etc. Material is copyright-free. "An essential part of any art library, and a book of permanent value," AMERICAN ARTIST. 212 plates. 224pp. 9 x 13¾. T20 Clothbound $10.00

*AN ATLAS OF ANATOMY FOR ARTISTS, F. Schider.* This standard work contains 189 full-page plates, more than 647 illustrations of all aspects of the human skeleton, musculature, cutaway portions of the body, each part of the anatomy, hand forms, eyelids, breasts, location of muscles under the flesh, etc. 59 plates illustrate how Michelangelo, da Vinci, Goya, 15 others, drew human anatomy. New 3rd edition enlarged by 52 new illustrations by Cloquet, Barcsay. "The standard reference tool," AMERICAN LIBRARY ASSOCIATION. "Excellent," AMERICAN ARTIST. 189 plates, 647 illustrations. xxvi + 192pp. 7⅞ x 10⅝. T241 Clothbound $6.00

*GREEK REVIVAL ARCHITECTURE IN AMERICA, T. Hamlin.* A comprehensive study of the American Classical Revival, its regional variations, reasons for its success and eventual decline. Profusely illustrated with photos, sketches, floor plans and sections, displaying the work of almost every important architect of the time. 2 appendices. 39 figures, 94 plates containing 221 photos, 62 architectural designs, drawings, etc. 324-item classified bibliography. Index. xi + 439pp. 5⅜ x 8½.

T1148 Paperbound $3.00

*CREATIVE LITHOGRAPHY AND HOW TO DO IT, Grant Arnold.* Written by a man who practiced and taught lithography for many years, this highly useful volume explains all the steps of the lithographic process from tracing the drawings on the stone to printing the lithograph, with helpful hints for solving special problems. Index. 16 reproductions of lithographs. 11 drawings. xv + 214pp. of text. 5⅜ x 8½.

T1208 Paperbound $1.65

*TEACH YOURSELF ANTIQUE COLLECTING, E. Bradford.* An excellent, brief guide to collecting British furniture, silver, pictures and prints, pewter, pottery and porcelain, Victoriana, enamels, clocks or other antiques. Much background information difficult to find elsewhere. 15pp. of illus. 215pp. 7 x 4¼.

Clothbound $2.00

*PAINTING IN THE FAR EAST, L. Binyon.* A study of over 1500 years of Oriental art by one of the world's outstanding authorities. The author chooses the most important masters in each period—Wu Tao-tzu, Toba Sojo, Kanaoka, Li Lung-mien, Masanobu, Okio, etc.—and examines the works, schools, and influence of each within their cultural context. 42 photographs. Sources of original works and selected bibliography. Notes including list of principal painters by periods. xx + 297pp. 6⅛ x 9¼.

T520 Paperbound $2.25

*THE ALPHABET AND ELEMENTS OF LETTERING, F. W. Goudy.* A beautifully illustrated volume on the aesthetics of letters and type faces and their history and development. Each plate consists of 15 forms of a single letter with the last plate devoted to the ampersand and the numerals. "A sound guide for all persons engaged in printing or drawing," Saturday Review. 27 full-page plates. 48 additional figures. xii + 131pp. 7⅞ x 10¾.

T792 Paperbound $2.00

*THE COMPLETE BOOK OF SILK SCREEN PRINTING PRODUCTION, J. I. Biegeleisen.* Here is a clear and complete picture of every aspect of silk screen technique and press operation—from individually operated manual presses to modern automatic ones. Unsurpassed as a guidebook for setting up shop, making shop operation more efficient, finding out about latest methods and equipment; or as a textbook for use in teaching, studying, or learning all aspects of the profession. 124 figures. Index. Bibliography. List of Supply Sources. xi + 253pp. 5⅜ x 8½.

T1100 Paperbound $2.00

*AN ATLAS OF ANIMAL ANATOMY FOR ARTISTS, W. Ellenberger, H. Baum, H. Dittrich.* The largest, richest animal anatomy for artists in English. Form, musculature, tendons, bone structure, expression, detailed cross sections of head, other features, of the horse, lion, dog, cat, deer, seal, kangaroo, cow, bull, goat, monkey, hare, many other animals. "Highly recommended," DESIGN. Second, revised, enlarged edition with new plates from Cuvier, Stubbs, etc. 288 illustrations. 153pp. 11⅜ x 9.

T82 Clothbound $6.00

*ANIMAL DRAWING: ANATOMY AND ACTION FOR ARTISTS, C. R. Knight.* 158 studies, with full accompanying text, of such animals as the gorilla, bear, bison, dromedary, camel, vulture, pelican, iguana, shark, etc., by one of the greatest modern masters of animal drawing. Innumerable tips on how to get life expression into your work. "An excellent reference work," SAN FRANCISCO CHRONICLE. 158 illustrations. 156pp. 10½ x 8½.

T426 Paperbound $2.00

*ARCHITECTURAL AND PERSPECTIVE DESIGNS, Giuseppe Galli Bibiena.* 50 imaginative scenic drawings of Giuseppe Galli Bibiena, principal theatrical engineer and architect to the Viennese court of Charles VI. Aside from its interest to art historians, students, and art lovers, there is a whole Baroque world of material in this book for the commercial artist. Portrait of Charles VI by Martin de Meytens. 1 allegorical plate. 50 additional plates. New introduction. vi + 103pp. 10⅛ x 13¼.

T1263 Paperbound $2.25

*HANDBOOK OF DESIGNS AND DEVICES, C. P. Hornung.* A remarkable working collection of 1836 basic designs and variations, all copyright-free. Variations of circle, line, cross, diamond, swastika, star, scroll, shield, many more. Notes on symbolism. "A necessity to every designer who would be original without having to labor heavily," ARTIST AND ADVERTISER. 204 plates. 240pp. 5⅜ x 8.

T125 Paperbound $1.90

*CHINESE HOUSEHOLD FURNITURE, G. N. Kates.* A summary of virtually everything that is known about authentic Chinese furniture before it was contaminated by the influence of the West. The text covers history of styles, materials used, principles of design and craftsmanship, and furniture arrangement—all fully illustrated. xiii + 190pp. 5⅝ x 8½.

T958 Paperbound $1.50

*DECORATIVE ART OF THE SOUTHWESTERN INDIANS, D. S. Sides.* 300 black and white reproductions from one of the most beautiful art traditions of the primitive world, ranging from the geometric art of the Great Pueblo period of the 13th century to modern folk art. Motives from basketry, beadwork, Zuni masks, Hopi kachina dolls, Navajo sand pictures and blankets, and ceramic ware. Unusual and imaginative designs will inspire craftsmen in all media, and commercial artists may reproduce any of them without permission or payment. xviii + 101pp. 5⅝ x 8⅜.

T139 Paperbound $1.00

*200 DECORATIVE TITLE-PAGES, edited by A. Nesbitt.* Fascinating and informative from a historical point of view, this beautiful collection of decorated titles will be a great inspiration to students of design, commercial artists, advertising designers, etc. A complete survey of the genre from the first known decorated title to work in the first decades of this century. Bibliography and sources of the plates. 222pp. 8⅜ x 11¼.

T1264 Paperbound $2.75

*ON THE LAWS OF JAPANESE PAINTING, H. P. Bowie.* This classic work on the philosophy and technique of Japanese art is based on the author's first-hand experiences studying art in Japan. Every aspect of Japanese painting is described: the use of the brush and other materials; laws governing conception and execution; subjects for Japanese paintings, etc. The best possible substitute for a series of lessons from a great Oriental master. Index. xv + 117pp. + 66 plates. 6⅛ x 9¼.

T30 Paperbound $2.00

*A HANDBOOK OF ANATOMY FOR ART STUDENTS, Arthur Thomson.* This long-popular text teaches any student, regardless of level of technical competence, all the subtleties of human anatomy. Clear photographs, numerous line sketches and diagrams of bones, joints, etc. Use it as a text for home study, as a supplement to life class work, or as a lifelong sourcebook and reference volume. Author's prefaces. 67 plates, containing 40 line drawings, 86 photographs—mostly full page. 211 figures. Appendix. Index. xx + 459pp. 5⅜ x 8⅜.  T1163 Paperbound $3.00

*WHITTLING AND WOODCARVING, E. J. Tangerman.* With this book, a beginner who is moderately handy can whittle or carve scores of useful objects, toys for children, gifts, or simply pass hours creatively and enjoyably. "Easy as well as instructive reading," N. Y. Herald Tribune Books. 464 illustrations, with appendix and index. x + 293pp. 5½ x 8⅛.

T965 Paperbound $1.75

*ONE HUNDRED AND ONE PATCHWORK PATTERNS, Ruby Short McKim.* Whether you have made a hundred quilts or none at all, you will find this the single most useful book on quiltmaking. There are 101 full patterns (all exact size) with full instructions for cutting and sewing. In addition there is some really choice folklore about the origin of the ingenious pattern names: "Monkey Wrench," "Road to California," "Drunkard's Path," "Crossed Canoes," to name a few. Over 500 illustrations. 124 pp. 7⅞ x 10¾.                    T773 Paperbound $1.85

*ART AND GEOMETRY, W. M. Ivins, Jr.* Challenges the idea that the foundations of modern thought were laid in ancient Greece. Pitting Greek tactile-muscular intuitions of space against modern visual intuitions, the author, for 30 years curator of prints, Metropolitan Museum of Art, analyzes the differences between ancient and Renaissance painting and sculpture and tells of the first fruitful investigations of perspective. x + 113pp. 5⅜ x 8⅜.                    T941 Paperbound $1.00

# Dover Books on Art

*LANDSCAPE GARDENING IN JAPAN, Josiah Conder.* A detailed picture of Japanese gardening techniques and ideas, the artistic principles incorporated in the Japanese garden, and the religious and ethical concepts at the heart of those principles. Preface. 92 illustrations, plus all 40 full-page plates from the Supplement. Index. xv + 299pp. 8⅜ x 11¼.

T1216 Paperbound $2.75

*DESIGN AND FIGURE CARVING, E. J. Tangerman.* "Anyone who can peel a potato can carve," states the author, and in this unusual book he shows you how, covering every stage in detail from very simple exercises working up to museum-quality pieces. Terrific aid for hobbyists, arts and crafts counselors, teachers, those who wish to make reproductions for the commercial market. Appendix: How to Enlarge a Design. Brief bibliography. Index. 1298 figures. x + 289pp. 5⅜ x 8½.

T1209 Paperbound $1.85

*THE STANDARD BOOK OF QUILT MAKING AND COLLECTING, M. Ickis.* Even if you are a beginner, you will soon find yourself quilting like an expert, by following these clearly drawn patterns, photographs, and step-by-step instructions. Learn how to plan the quilt, to select the pattern to harmonize with the design and color of the room, to choose materials. Over 40 full-size patterns. Index. 483 illustrations. One color plate. xi + 276pp 6¾ x 9½.

T582 Paperbound $2.00

*LOST EXAMPLES OF COLONIAL ARCHITECTURE, J. M. Howells.* This book offers a unique guided tour through America's architectural past, all of which is either no longer in existence or so changed that its original beauty has been destroyed. More than 275 clear photos of old churches, dwelling houses, public buildings, business structures, etc. 245 plates, containing 281 photos and 9 drawings, floorplans, etc. New Index. xvii + 248pp. 7⅞ x 10¾.

T1143 Paperbound $2.75

*A HISTORY OF COSTUME, Carl Köhler.* The most reliable and authentic account of the development of dress from ancient times through the 19th century. Based on actual pieces of clothing that have survived, using paintings, statues and other reproductions only where originals no longer exist. Hundreds of illustrations, including detailed patterns for many articles. Highly useful for theatre and movie directors, fashion designers, illustrators, teachers. Edited and augmented by Emma von Sichart. Translated by Alexander K. Dallas. 594 illustrations. 464pp. 5⅛ x 7⅛.

T1030 Paperbound $2.75

*Dover publishes books on commercial art, art history, crafts, design, art classics; also books on music, literature, science, mathematics, puzzles and entertainments, chess, engineering, biology, philosophy, psychology, languages, history, and other fields. For free circulars write to Dept. DA, Dover Publications, Inc., 180 Varick St., New York, N.Y. 10014.*